Alternate Problems
Volume II, Chapter 15-25

for use with

Financial and Managerial Accounting
The Basis for Business Decisions

Twelfth Edition

Jan R. Williams
University of Tennessee-Knoxville

Susan F. Haka
Michigan State University

Mark S. Bettner
Bucknell University

Robert F. Meigs
San Diego State University

Prepared by
Robert Zwicker
Pace University

Boston   Burr Ridge, IL   Dubuque, IA   Madison, WI   New York   San Francisco   St. Louis
Bangkok   Bogotá   Caracas   Kuala Lumpur   Lisbon   London   Madrid   Mexico City
Milan   Montreal   New Delhi   Santiago   Seoul   Singapore   Sydney   Taipei   Toronto

McGraw-Hill Higher Education

A Division of The McGraw·Hill Companies

Alternate Problems, Volume II, Chapters 15-25 for use with
FINANCIAL AND MANAGERIAL ACCOUNTING: THE BASIS FOR BUSINESS DECISIONS
Williams, Haka, Bettner, and Meigs

Published by McGraw-Hill/Irwin, an imprint of the McGraw-Hill Companies, Inc., 1221 Avenue of the Americas, New York, NY 10020. Copyright © 2002 by the McGraw-Hill Companies, Inc. All rights reserved. No part of this publication may be reproduced or distributed in any form or by any means, or stored in a database or retrieval system, without the prior written consent of The McGraw-Hill Companies, Inc., including, but not limited to, in any network or other electronic storage or transmission, or broadcast for distance learning.

1 2 3 4 5 6 7 8 9 0 BKM/BKM 0 9 8 7 6 5 4 3 2 1

ISBN 0-07-250319-X

www.mhhe.com

Table of Contents

Chapter 15: Global Business and Accounting 15-1

Chapter 16: Management Accounting: A Business Partner 16-1

Chapter 17: Accounting Systems for Measuring Costs 17-1

Chapter 18: Costing and the Value Chain 18-1

Chapter 19: Cost-Volume-Profit Analysis 19-1

Chapter 20: Incremental Analysis 20-1

Chapter 21: Responsibility Accounting and Transfer Pricing 21-1

Chapter 22: Operational Budgeting 22-1

Chapter 23: Standard Cost Systems 23-1

Chapter 24: Rewarding Business Performance 24-1

Chapter 25: Capital Budgeting 25-1

CHAPTER 15 ALTERNATE PROBLEMS

Problem 15.1A
Exchange Rates and Export Decision

The Monster Cookie Company is located in Denmark. It is a relatively new company and so far has sold its products only in its home country. In December, Monster determined that it had excess capacity to produce more of its special Halloween cookies. It is trying to decide whether to use that capacity to ship a batch of cookies overseas. The marketing department has determined that the United States and Great Britain are the two most viable markets. Monster has enough excess capacity to produce only one batch, which can be shipped to either country. The materials and labor cost to produce the batch amount to $9,000 kroner. The marketing department, which located a shipping company that could deliver to either location, also provided the following information:

	United States	Great Britain
Shipping cost	2,800 U.S. dollars	1,900 U.S. dollars
Duties/customs charges and miscellaneous selling expenses	420 U.S. dollars	500 British pounds
Total sales revenue	6,000 U.S. dollars	2,600 British pounds
Exchange rate data	1 krone = 0.16 U.S. dollars	1 krone = 0.09 British pounds

Instructions
a. If Monster exports the batch to the United States, what is its estimated profit/loss in Danish kroner?
b. If Monster exports the batch to Great Britain, what is its estimated profit/loss in Danish kroner?
c. If the British pound has exhibited rather large fluctuations relative to the Danish kroner recently, how might this impact Monster's decision on which country to ship to?

Problem 15.2A
Gains and Losses from Exchange Rate Fluctuations

Euroam is a U.S. corporation that purchases tractors from European manufacturers for distribution in the United States. A recent purchase involved the following events:

Dec. 1 Purchased tractors from WMB Motors for DM4,000,000, payable in 45 days. Current exchange rate, $0.75 per deutsche mark. (Euroam uses the perpetual inventory system.)

Dec. 31 Made year-end adjusting entry relating to the DM4,000,000 account payable to WMB Motors. Current exchange rate, $0.78 per deutsche mark.

Jan. 15 Issued a check to World Bank for $3,080,000 in full payment of the account payable to WMB Motors.

Instructions
a. Prepare in general journal form the entries necessary to record the preceding events.
b. Compute the exchange rate (price) of the deutsche mark in U.S. dollars on January 15.
c. Explain a hedging technique that Euroam might have used to protect itself from the possibility of losses resulting from a significant increase in the exchange rate for the deutsche mark.

Problem 15.3A
Exchange Rates and Income Effects

Jelton, Inc., is a U.S. company that conducts some business in Canada. The pro forma income statement for next year is shown below. Jelton wants to know the impact of three possible exchange rate scenarios for the Canadian dollar on its pro forma income statement: Assume one Canadian dollar is equivalent to either $0.70, $0.80, or $0.90 in U.S. dollars. Note that Jelton's sales in the United States are higher when the Canadian dollar is stronger because Canadian competitors are priced out of the U.S. market.

JELTON, INC.
Pro Forma Income Statement
For the Period Ending December 31, 2002

	U.S. Business	Canadian Business
Sales	$400.00	C$ 5
Cost of Goods Sold	100.00	100
Gross Profit	**$300.00**	**C$(95)**
Operating Expenses:		
Fixed	40.00	-0-
Variable	30.00	-0-
Total	$70.00	-0-
Operating Earnings	$230.00	C$ (95)
Interest Expenses	5.00	10
Earnings Before Tax	**$225.00**	**C$(105)**

Additional Information

Possible Exchange Rate	Projected U.S. Sales
$0.70	$395
0.80	400
0.90	405

Instructions

    a. Complete the chart in the working papers related to the following pro forma income statements in U.S. dollars:

	C$ = $0.70	C$ = $0.80	C$ = 0.90
Sales:			
(1) U.S.			
(2) Canadian			
(3) Total			
Cost of Goods Sold			
(4) U.S.			
(5) Canadian			
(6) Total			
(7) Gross Profit		$224.00	
Operating Expenses:			
(8) U.S. Fixed			
(9) U.S. Variable			
10% of Sales			
(10) Total			
(11) Operating Earnings			$138.55
Interest Expenses:			
(12) U.S.			
(13) Canadian			
(14) Total			
Earnings Before Tax	$136.65		

    b. Explain the impact of a stronger Canadian dollar on Earnings Before Tax.

Problem 15.4A
Exchange Rates and Product Decisions

The ALSU Company has manufacturing subsidiaries in Malaysia and Malta. It is considering shipping the subscomponents of Product X to one or the other of these countries for final assembly. The final product will be sold in the country where it is assembled. Other information is as follows:

	Malaysia	Malta
Average exchange rate	$1 = 4.50 ringgit	$1 = 0.40 lira
Import duty	4%	12%
Income tax rate	25%	12%
Unit selling price of Product X	700 ringgit	75 lira
Price of subcomponent	200 ringgit	18 lira
Final assembly costs	250 ringgit	30 lira
Number of units to be sold	14,000 units	10,000 units

In both countries, the import duties are based on the value of the incoming goods in the receiving country's currency.

Instructions
a. For each country, prepare an income statement on a per-unit basis denominated in that country's currency.
b. In which country would the highest profit per unit (in dollars) be earned?
c. In which country would the highest total profit (in dollars) be earned?

Problem 15.5A
A Comprehensive Problem on Exchange Rate Fluctuations

Fox Radio is a U.S. company that manufacturers radios. Many of the components for the computer are purchased abroad, and the finished product is sold in foreign countries as well as in the United States. Among the recent transactions of Fox are the following:

Oct. 25   Purchased from Sutaki, a Japanese company, 15,000 tubes. The purchase price was ¥120,000,000, payable in 30 days. Current exchange rate , $0.01 per yen. (Fox uses the perpetual inventory method; debit the Inventory of Raw Materials account.)

Nov. 15   Sold 500 radios to the British Vibes for £200,000 due in 30 days. The cost of the computers, to be debited to the Cost of Goods Sold account, was $160,000. Current exchange rate, $1.60 per British pound. (Use one compound journal entry to record the sale and the cost of goods sold. In recording the cost of goods sold, credit Inventory of Finished Goods.)

Nov. 24   Issued a check to Inland Bank for $1,150,000 in *full payment* of account payable to Sutaki.

Dec. 4   Purchased 5,000 black cases from German Plastics for DM80,000, payable in 60 days. Current exchange rate, $0.70 per deutsche mark. (Debit Inventory of Raw Materials.)

Dec. 15   Collected dollar-equivalent of £200,000 from the British Vibes. Current exchange rate, $1.55 per British pound.

Dec. 11   Sold 6,000 radios to Sounds, a French retail chain, for FF40,000,000, due in 30 days. Current exchange rate, $0.20 per French franc. The cost of the computers, to be debited to Cost of Goods Sold and credited to Inventory of Finished Goods, is $5,000,000.

Instructions
a. Prepare in general journal form the entries necessary to record the preceding transactions.
b. Prepare the adjusted entries needed at December 31 for the DM80,000 account payable to German Plastics and the FF40,000,000 account receivable from Sounds. Year-end exchange rates, $0.68 per deutsche mark and $0.18 per French franc. (Use a separate journal entry to adjust each account balance.)
c. Compute (to the nearest dollar) the unit sales price of computers in U.S. dollars in both the November 15 and the December 11 sales transaction. (The sales price may not be the same in each transaction.)
d. Compute the exchange rate for the yen, stated in U.S. dollars, on November 24.
e. Explain how Fox Radio could have hedged its position to reduce the risk of loss from exchange rate fluctuations on (1) its foreign payables and (2) its foreign receivables.

CHAPTER 16 ALTERNATE PROBLEMS

Problem 16.1A
An Introduction to Product Costs

Pisna, Inc. manufactures dowhats. The manufacturing costs incurred during its first year of operations are shown as follows:

Direct materials purchased...	$400,000
Direct materials used...	385,000
Direct labor assigned to production	350,000
Manufacturing overhead	425,000
Cost of finished goods manufactured (100 dowhats)	900,000

During the year, 100 completed dowhats were manufactured, of which 90 were sold. (Assume the amount of the ending inventory of finished goods and the cost of goods sold are determined using the average-per-unit cost of manufacturing a completed dowhat.

Instructions
a. Compute each of the following and show all computations:
   1. The average per-unit cost of manufacturing a completed dowhat during the current year.
   2. The year-end balances of the inventories of materials, work in progress, and finished goods.
   3. The cost of goods sold during the year.
b. For the current year, the costs of direct materials purchased, direct labor assigned to production, and actual manufacturing overhead total $1,175,000. Is this the amount of manufacturing costs deducted from revenue in the current year? Explain fully.

Alternate Problems for use with Financial and Managerial Accounting, 12e

Problem 16.2A
An Introduction to Product Costs

River Queen Corporation began operations early in the current year, building luxury boats. During the year, the company started and completed 40 boats at a cost of $80,000 per unit. Of these, 30 were sold for $130,000 each and ten remain in finished goods inventory. In addition, the company had five partially completed units in its factory at year-end. Total costs for the year (summarized alphabetically) were as follows:

Direct materials used..	$ 800,000
Direct labor applied to production...	1,000,000
Income taxes expense...	80,000
General and administrative expenses...	600,000
Manufacturing overhead..	2,000,000
Selling expenses...	400,000

Instructions
Compute the following for the current year:
- **a.** Total manufacturing costs charged to work in process during the period.
- **b.** Cost of finished goods manufactured.
- **c.** Cost of goods sold.
- **d.** Gross profit on sales.
- **e.** Ending inventories of (1) work in process and (2) finished goods.

Problem 16.3A
The Flow of Manufacturing Costs Through Ledger Accounts

The flow of manufacturing costs through the ledger accounts of Inferior Safes, Inc., in the current year is illustrated below in summarized form:

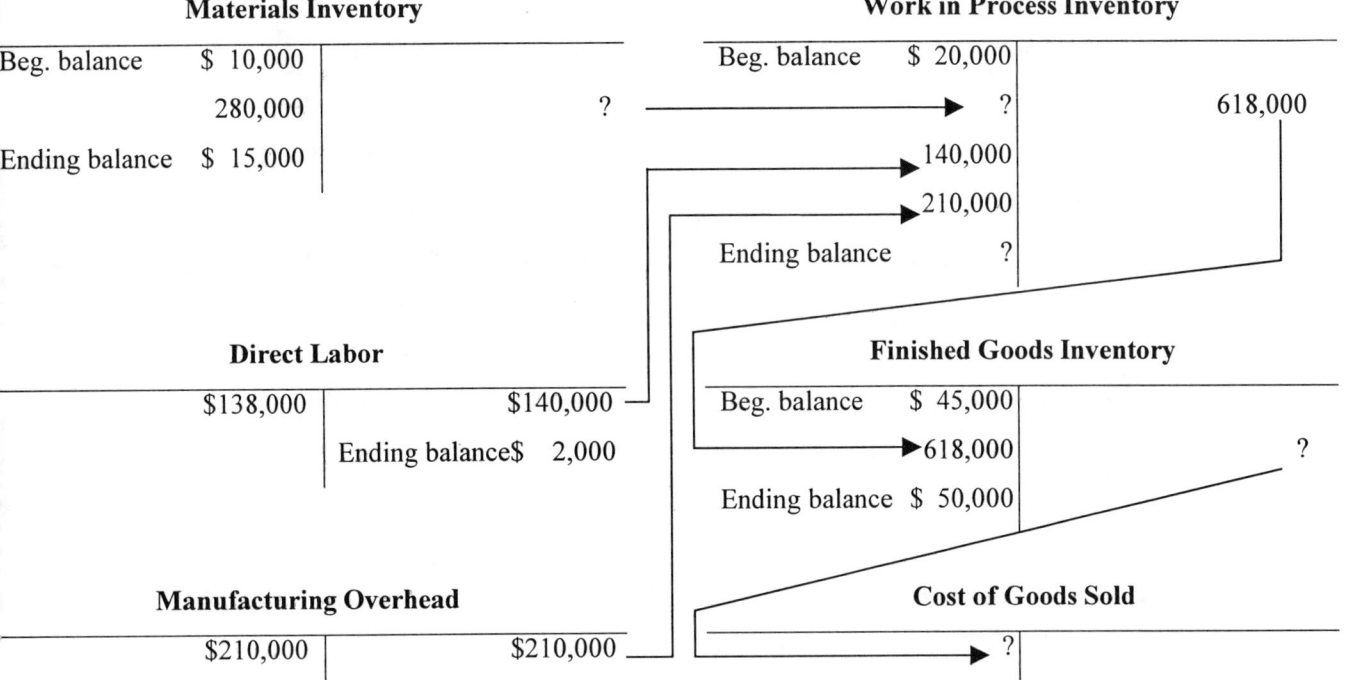

Instructions
Indicate the amounts requested below. Some amounts are shown in the T accounts above; others require short computations. (Show all computations.)

- **a.** Purchases of direct materials.
- **b.** The cost of direct materials used.
- **c.** Direct labor costs assigned to production.
- **d.** The year-end liability for direct wages payable.
- **e.** The overhead application rate in use throughout the year, assuming that overhead is applied as a percentage of direct labor costs.
- **f.** Total manufacturing costs charged to the Work in Process Inventory account during the current year.
- **g.** The cost of finished goods manufactured.
- **h.** The year-end balance in the Work in Progress Inventory account.
- **i.** The cost of goods sold.
- **j.** The total amount of inventory listed in the year-end balance sheet.

Problem 16.4A
The Flow of Manufacturing Costs Through Perpetual Inventory Records

The following T accounts summarize the flow of manufacturing costs during the current year through the ledger accounts of Payback Corporation:

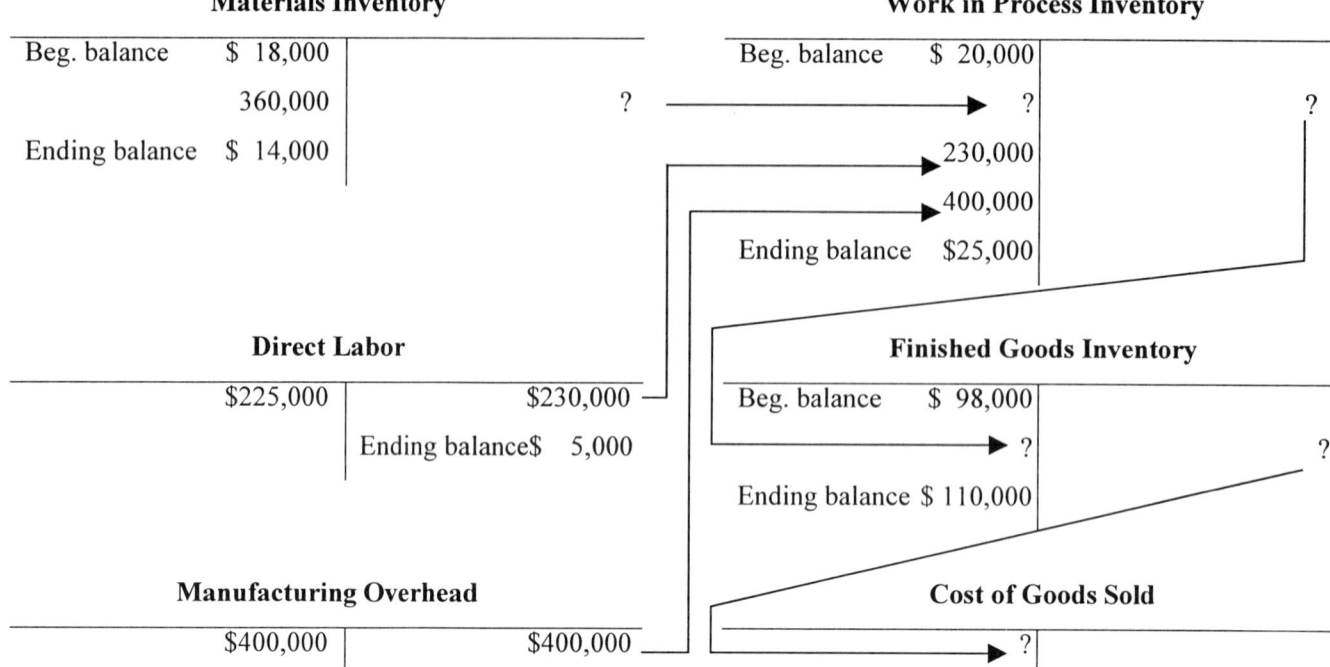

Instructions
From the data supplied above, indicate the following amounts. Some amounts are shown in the T accounts above; others require short computations. (Show all computations.)
    a. Purchases during the year of direct materials.
    b. The cost of direct materials used.
    c. Direct labor payrolls paid during the year.
    d. Direct labor costs assigned to production.
    e. The overhead application rate in use throughout the year, assuming that overhead is applied as a percentage of direct labor costs.
    f. Total manufacturing costs charged to the Work in Process Inventory account during the current year.
    g. The cost of finished goods manufactured.
    h. The cost of goods sold.
    i. The total costs to be classified as inventory in the year-end balance sheet.

Problem 16.5A
The Flow of Manufacturing Costs: A Comprehensive Problem

The balances in the perpetual inventory accounts of Mountainside Manufacturing Corporation at the beginning and end of the current year are as follows:

	End of Year	Beginning of Year
Inventory accounts:		
Materials	$30,000	$25,000
Work in Process	10,000	8,000
Finished Goods Inventory	29,000	30,000

Total dollar amounts debited and credited during the year to the accounts used in recording manufacturing activities are as follows:

	Debit Entries	Credit Entries
Account:		
Materials Inventory	$425,000	$?
Direct Labor	200,000	210,000
Manufacturing Overhead	420,000	420,000
Work in Process Inventory	?	?
Finished Goods Inventory	?	?

Instructions
a. Using these data, state or compute for the year the following amounts:
  1. Direct materials purchased.
  2. Direct materials used.
  3. Payments of direct labor payrolls.
  4. Direct labor cost assigned to production.
  5. The overhead application rate used during the year, assuming that overhead was applied as a percentage of direct labor costs.
  6. Total manufacturing costs charged to the Work in Process Inventory account during the year.
  7. The cost of finished goods manufactured.
  8. The cost of goods sold.
  9. The total amount to be classified as inventory in the year-end balance sheet.
b. Prepare a schedule of the cost of finished goods manufactured.

Problem 16.6A
Determining and Reporting Product Cost Information

The following are 2002 data regarding Old Joe, one of the major products manufactured by the Columbus Toy Company:

Purchases of direct materials	$400,000
Direct materials used	402,000
Direct labor payrolls (paid during the year)	180,000
Direct labor costs assigned to production	220,000
Manufacturing overhead (incurred and applied)	330,000

During the year 50,000 units of this product were manufactured and 51,500 units were sold. Selected information concerning inventories during the year follows:

	Dec. 31	Jan. 1
Materials	$?	$15,000
Work in Process	6,000	5,000
Finished Goods, Jan. 1 (4,000 units $19)	?	76,000

Instructions

a. Prepare a schedule of the cost of finished goods manufactured for the Old Joe product in 2002.
b. Compute the average cost of Old Joe completed 2002.
c. Compute the cost of goods sold associated with the sale of Old Joe in 2002. Assume that there is a first-in, first-out (FIFO) flow through the Finished Goods Inventory account and that all units completed in 2002 are assigned the per-unit costs determined in part **b**.
d. Compute the amount of inventory relating to Old Joe that will be listed in the company's balance sheet at December 31, 2002. Show supporting computations for the year-end amounts of materials inventory and finished goods inventory.
e. Explain where the $180,000 in direct labor costs assigned to production in 2002 affect the company's 2002 income statement and balance sheet.

Problem 16.7A
Determining and Reporting Product Cost Information

The following are the beginning and ending balances in the inventory accounts of Al's Parts for 2002:

	End of Year	Beginning of Year
Inventory accounts:		
Materials	$47,000	$42,000
Work in Process	35,000	38,000
Finished Goods Inventory	?	105,000

The amounts debited and credited during the year to the accounts used in recording manufacturing costs are as follows:

	Debit Entries	Credit Entries
Account:		
Materials Inventory	$ 910,000	$?
Direct Labor	405,000	410,000
Manufacturing Overhead	1,100,000	1,100,000
Cost of Goods Sold	2,340,000	-0-
Work in Process Inventory	?	?
Finished Goods Inventory	?	?

Instructions
a. Using the given information data, state or compute for the 2002 the following amounts:
   1. Direct materials purchased.
   2. Direct materials used.
   3. Direct labor payrolls paid during the year.
   4. Direct labor costs assigned to units being manufactured.
   5. The year-end liability for direct wages payable.
   6. The overhead application rate, assuming that overhead costs are applied to units being manufactured using 22,000 direct labor hours as an estimated activity base.
   7. Total manufacturing costs debited to the Work in Process Inventory account.
   8. Cost of finished goods manufactured.
   9. Ending inventory of finished goods.
b. Prepare a schedule of the cost of finished goods manufactured.

Problem 16.8A
Determining Unit Costs Using the Cost of Finished Goods Manufactured

The accounting records of the Maine Products Company include the following information relating to the current year:

	Dec. 31	Jan. 31
Materials inventory	$ 22,000	$ 30,000
Work in process inventory	39,000	39,000
Finished goods inventory, Jan. 1 (8,000 units @ 22 per unit)	?	176,000
Purchases of direct materials during year	290,000	
Direct labor costs assigned to production	350,000	
Manufacturing overhead applied to production	552,000	

The company manufactures a single product; during the current year, 60,000 units were manufactured and 50,000 units were sold.

Instructions

a. Prepares a schedule of the cost of finished goods manufactured for the current year. (Show a supporting computation of the cost of direct materials *used* during the year.)
b. Compute the average per-unit cost of production during the year.
c. Compute the cost of goods sold during the year, assuming that the FIFO (first-in, first-out) method of inventory costing is used.
d. Compute the cost of the inventory of finished goods at December 31 of the current year, assuming that the FIFO (first-in, first-out) method of inventory costing is used.

Problem 16.9A
Preparing an Income Statement Using the Cost of Finished Goods Manufactured

Sallyton Company, a sole proprietorship, reports the following information pertaining to its 2002 operating activities:

	12/31/02 Balance	1/1/02 Balance
Materials Inventory	$25,000	$32,000
Work in Process Inventory	33,000	58,000
Finished Goods Inventory	70,000	60,000

During the year, the company purchased $40,000 of direct materials and incurred $32,000 of direct labor costs. Total manufacturing overhead costs for the year amounted to $20,000. Selling and administrative expenses amounted to $55,000, and the company's annual sales amounted to $250,000

Instruction
a. Prepare Sallyton's schedule of the cost of finished goods manufactured for 2002.
b. Prepare Sallyton's 2002 income statement (ignore income taxes).

Problem 16.10A
Preparing an Income Statement Using the Cost of Finished Goods Manufactured

Valley Company reports the following information pertaining to its 2002 operating activities:

	12/31/02 Balance	1/1/02 Balance
Materials Inventory	$62,000	$55,000
Work in Process Inventory	40,000	30,000
Finished Goods Inventory	18,000	22,000

During the year, the company purchased $42,000 of direct materials and incurred $32,000 of direct labor costs. Total manufacturing overhead costs for the year amounted to $20,000. Selling and administrative expenses amounted to $32,000, and the company's annual sales amounted to $95,000

Instruction
a. Prepare Ridgeway's schedule of the cost of finished goods manufactured for 2002.
b. Prepare Ridgeway's 2002 income statement (ignore income taxes).

Problem 16.11A
Measuring Unit Cost

Early in the year, Bill Edmond founded Edmond Engineering Co. for the purpose of manufacturing a special plumbing device that he had designed. Shortly after year-end, the company's accountant was injured in an auto accident, and no year-end financial statements have been prepared. However, the accountant had correctly determined the year-end inventories at the following amounts:

Materials	$52,000
Work in process	32,000
Finished goods (4,000 units)	91,000

As this was the first year of operations, there were no beginnings of inventories.

While the accountant was in the hospital, Edmond improperly prepared the following income statement from the company's accounting records:

Net sales		$625,000
Cost of goods sold:		
Purchases of direct materials	$185,000	
Direct labor costs assigned to production	115,000	
Manufacturing overhead applied to production	160,000	
Selling expenses	75,000	
Administrative expenses	135,000	
Total costs		670,000
Net loss for year		$(45,000)

Edmonds was very disappointed in these operating results. He states, "Not only did we lose more than $40,000 this year, but look at our unit production costs. We sold 10,000 units this year at a cost of $670,000; that amounts to a cost of $67 per unit. I know some of our competitors are able to manufacture similar valves for about $30 per unit. I don't need an accountant to know that this business is a failure."

Instructions
a. Prepare a schedule of the cost of finished goods manufactured for the year. (As there were no beginning inventories, your schedule will start with "Manufacturing costs assigned to production:." Show a supporting computation for the cost of direct materials used during the year.
b. Compute the average cost per unit manufactured.
c. Prepare a corrected income statement for the year, using the multiple-step format. If the company has earned any operating income, assume an income tax rate of 20%. (Omit earnings per share figures.)
d. Explain whether you agree or disagree with Edmond's remarks that the business is unprofitable and that its unit cost of production ($67, according to Edmond) is much higher than that of competitors (around $30). If you disagree with Edmond, explain any errors or shortcomings in his analysis.

Problem 16.12A
Effect on Income Statement of Errors in Handling Manufacturing Costs

John Bronx, the chief accountant of NY Banjo Company, was injured in an automobile accident shortly before the end of the company's first year of operations. At year-end, a clerk with a very limited understanding of accounting prepared the following income statement, which is unsatisfactory in several respects:

NY BANJO COMPANY
Income Statement
For the Year Ended December 31, 20__

Net sales		$1,250,000
Cost of goods sold:		
Purchases of direct materials	$430,000	
Direct labor	200,000	
Indirect labor	100,000	
Depreciation on machinery – factory	40,000	
Rent	130,000	
Insurance	20,000	
Utilities	30,000	
Miscellaneous manufacturing overhead	50,000	
Other operating expenses	300,000	
Dividends declared on capital stock	40,000	
Cost of goods sold		$1,340,000
Loss for year		(90,000)

You are asked to help management prepare a corrected income statement for the first year of operations. Management informs you that 70% of the rent, insurance, and utilities applies to factory operations, and that the remaining 30% should be classified as period expense. Also, the correct ending inventories are as follows:

Material	$ 50,000
Work in process	30,000
Finished goods	125,000

As this is the first year of operations, there were no beginning inventories.

Instructions

a. Identify the shortcomings and errors in the above income statement. Based on the shortcomings you have identified, explain whether you would expect the company's actual net income for the first year of operations to be higher or lower than the amount shown.
b. Prepare schedules to determine:
   1. The cost of direct materials used.
   2. Total manufacturing overhead.
c. Prepare a schedule of cost of finished goods manufactured during the year. (Use the amounts computed in part **b** as the costs of direct materials used and manufacturing overhead.)
d. Prepare a corrected income statement for the year, using a multiple-step format. Assume that income taxes expense amounts to 25% of income before income taxes.

CHAPTER 17 ALTERNATE PROBLEMS

Problem 17.1A
Job Order Costing Computations and Journal Entries

Nanik Boat, Inc. uses job order costing. Manufacturing overhead is charged to individual jobs through the use of a predetermined overhead rate based on direct labor costs. The following information appears in the company's Work in Progress Inventory controlling account for the month August.

Debits to account:	
Balance, August 1	$ 8,000
Direct materials	14,000
Direct labor	10,000
Manufacturing overhead (applied to jobs as 200% of direct labor cost)	20,000
Total debits to account	$52,000
Credits to account:	
Transferred to Finished Goods Inventory account	40,000
Balanced, August 31	$ 12,000

Instructions
a. Assuming that the direct labor charged to the jobs still in process at August 31 amounts to $3,200, compute the amount of manufacturing overhead and the amount of direct materials that have been charged to these jobs as of August 31.
b. Prepare general journal entries to summarize:
   1. The manufacturing costs (direct materials, direct labor, and overhead) charged to production during August.
   2. The transfer of production completed during August to the Finished Goods Inventory account.
   3. The cash sale of 85% of the merchandise completed during August at a total sales price of $50,000. Show the related cost of goods sold in a separate journal entry.

Problem 17.2A
Job Order Costing: Journal Entries and Cost Flows

The following information relates to the manufacturing operations of Dello Mfg. Co. during the month of April. The company uses job order costing.

a. Purchases of direct materials during the month amount of $72,000. (All purchases were made on account.)
b. Materials requisitions issued by the Production Department during the month total $68,300.
c. Time cards of direct workers show 1,800 hours worked on various jobs during the month, for a total direct labor cost of $35,000.
d. Direct workers were paid $33,000 in April.
e. Actual overhead costs for the month amount to $41,000 (for simplicity, you may credit Accounts Payable).
f. Overhead is applied to jobs at a rate of $22 per direct labor hour.
g. Jobs with total accumulated costs of $97,000 were completed during the month.
h. During April, units costing $80,000 were sold for $170,000. (All sales were made on account.)

Instructions

Prepare general journal entries to summarize each of these transactions in the company's general ledger accounts.

Problem 17.3A
Job Order Costing: A Comprehensive Problem

Kansas Plains, Inc., manufactures heavy equipment to customers' specifications and uses job order costing. A predetermined overhead rate is used in applying manufacturing overhead to individual jobs. In Department One, overhead is applied on the basis of machine-hours, and in Department Two, on the basis of direct labor hours. At the beginning of the current year, management made the following budget estimates to assist in determining the overhead application rate.

	Department One	Department Two
Direct labor cost	$420,000	$308,000
Direct labor hours	30,000	20,000
Manufacturing overhead	630,000	500,000
Machine-hours	10,000	5,000

Production of a batch of custom furniture ordered by Blan, Inc. (job no. 41) was started early in the year and completed two weeks later on January 19). The records for this job show the following cost information:

	Department One	Department Two
Job order for Blan, Inc. (job no. 41):		
Direct materials cost	$ 8,300	$5,000
Direct labor cost	12,000	9,000
Direct labor hours	800	400
Machine-hours	600	300

Selected additional information for January is as follows:

	Department One	Department Two
Direct labor hours – month of January	$ 2,000	$1,800
Machine-hours – month of January	1,500	1,000
Manufacturing overhead incurred in January	96,000	40,000

Instructions
a. Compute the predetermined overhead rate for each department.
b. What is the total cost of the equipment produced for Blan, Inc.
c. Prepare the entries required to record the sale (on account) of the equipment to Blan, Inc. The sales price of the order was $150,000.
d. Determine the over- or underapplied overhead for each department at the end of January.

Problem 17.4A
Job Order Costing: A Comprehensive Problem

Dot, Inc. uses job order costing and applies manufacturing overhead to individual jobs by using predetermined overhead rates. In Department A, overhead is applied on the basis of machine hours, and in Department B, on the basis of direct labor hours. At the beginning of the current year, management made the following budget estimates as a step toward determining the overhead application rates:

	Department A	Department B
Direct labor	$500,000	$360,000
Manufacturing overhead	600,000	432,000
Machine-hours	20,000	1,000
Direct labor hours	30,000	21,600

Production of 2,000 tachometers (job no. XL), was started in the middle of January and completed two weeks later. The cost records for this job show the following information:

	Department A	Department B
Job no. XL (2,000 units of product):		
Cost of materials used on job	$7,200	$5,200
Direct labor cost	5,000	6,666
Direct labor hours	300	400
Machine-hours	100	200

Instructions

a. Determine the overhead rate that should be used for each department in applying overhead costs to job no. XL.
b. What is the total cost of job no. XL, and what is the unit cost of the product manufactured on this production order?
c. Prepare the journal entries required to record the sale (on account) of 1,000 units. The total sales price was $22,000.
d. Assume that actual overhead costs for the year were $470,000 in Department A and $490,000 in Department B. Actual machine-hours in Department A were $15,000, and actual direct labor hours in Department B were 25,000 during the year. On the basis of this information, determine the over- or underapplied overhead in each department for the year.

Problem 17.5A
Process Costing

The Yellow Pine Furniture Company produces tables in two departments. Assembly and Finishing. In the Assembly Department, all direct materials (wood) are entered into production at the start of the process. Various machines cut the raw wood into appropriate pieces and workers assemble the pieces into tables. Thus, in the Assembly Department, all direct labor and overhead is incurred evenly throughout the process. The Finishing Department then takes the tables, applies numerous coats of stain and varnish, and finally buffs and packages the completed tables. Thus, in the Finishing Department, direct materials are added evenly throughout the first half of the process, while the direct labor is added evenly throughout the last half. Overhead is incurred evenly over the entire finishing process. Yellow Pine uses process costing and had the following cost and production information available for January, its first month of operation:

	Assembly Department	Finishing Department
Direct materials cost	$32,000	$ 8,200
Direct labor cost	12,000	16,000
Manufacturing overhead applied	15,000	8,400
Total manufacturing costs	$59,000	$32,600
Units in beginning work in process	0	0
Units started	800	600
Units completed and transferred out	600	450
Units in ending work in process	200	150
Percentage complete – ending work in process	30%	60%

During the month of January, 380 tables were sold and shipped to customers at a retail price of $400 each.

Instructions

a. For January, calculate the equivalent units produced by the Assembly Department and the Finishing Department for the three cost categories – direct materials, direct labor, and manufacturing overhead.
b. Calculate the assembly, finishing, and total cost of producing a table during January.
c. For the month of January, prepare the journal entries summarizing the manufacturing costs charged to the Assembly Department and the Finishing Department.
d. For January, prepare the month-end journal entries to transfer the costs of tables moved from the Assembly Department to the Finishing Department and from the Finishing Department to Finished Goods Inventory.
e. Prepare the entries to record the sales made in January and the corresponding reduction at Finished Goods Inventory.
f. Using T accounts, calculate the ending balances in the Work in Process accounts and Finished Goods Inventory.

Problem 17.6A
Process Costing

Quaker Co. makes oatmeal cookies. The cookies pass through three production processes: mixing the cookie dough, baking, and packaging. Quaker uses process costing.

The following are data concerning the costs incurred in each process during June along with the number of units processed:

	Mixing	Baking	Packaging
Direct materials	$4,200	$ 0	$2,000
Direct labor	2,500	2,000	4,000
Manufacturing overhead	7,500	6,000	1,000
Output	12,000 lb	3,000 gross*	36,000 boxes

*A gross is 12 dozen.

To ensure freshness, cookies are baked and packaged on the same day that the dough is mixed. Thus the company has no inventory still in process at the end of a business day.

Instructions

a. Prepare a separate journal entry summarizing the costs incurred by the Mixing Department in preparing 12,000 pounds of cookie dough in June. In the explanation of you entry, indicate the department's unit cost. (Round to nearest penny.)
b. Prepare the month-end entry recording the transfer of cookie dough to the Baking Department during May.
c. Prepare a journal entry summarizing the costs incurred by the Baking Department in May (excluding the costs transferred from the Mixing Department). In the explanation, indicate the *cost per gross* of the baking process. (Round to the nearest penny.)
d. Prepare the month-end entry recording the transfer of cookies from the Baking Department to the Packaging Department in May.
e. Prepare a journal entry summarizing the costs incurred by the Packaging Department in May. In the explanation, indicate the packaging cost per box. (Round to the nearest penny.)
f. Prepare the month-end entry to record the transfers in May of cases of cookies from the Packaging Department to the finished goods warehouse. In the explanation, indicate the total cost per box transferred. (Round to the nearest penny.)
g. Briefly explain how the management will use the unit cost information appearing in the entries **a, c, e,** and **f**.

Problem 17.7A
Applying Overhead Costs Using ABD

Kramden Chemical Company produce two products: Aoxide and Boxide. The company uses activity-based costing (ABC) to allocate manufacturing overhead to these products. The costs incurred by Kramden's Purchasing Department average $100,000 per year and constitute a major portion of the company's total manufacturing overhead.

Purchasing Department costs are assigned to two activity cost pools: (1) to order cost pool and (2) the inspection cost pool. Costs are assigned to the pools based on the number of employees engaged in each activity. Of the department's five full-time employees, two are responsible for ordering raw materials, and three are responsible for inspecting incoming shipments of materials.

Costs assigned to the order pool are allocated to products based on the total number of purchase orders generated by each product line. Costs assigned to the inspection pool are allocated to products based on the number of inspections related to each product line.

For the upcoming year, Kramden estimates the following activity levels:

	Total	Aoxide	Boxide
Purchase orders generated..................	10,000	3,000	7,000
Inspections conducted........................	2,000	1,600	400

In a normal year, the company conducts 2,000 inspections to sample the quantity of raw materials. The large number of Aoxide related inspections is due to quality problems experiences in the past. The quality of Boxide materials has been consistently good.

Instructions
a. Assign the Purchasing Department's costs to the individual cost pools.
b. Allocate the order cost pool to the individual product lines.
c. Allocate the inspection cost pool to the individual product lines.
d. Suggest how Kramden might reduce manufacturing costs incurred by the Purchasing Department.

Problem 17.8A
ABC Versus Use of a Single Activity Base

Mason Robotics manufactures three robot models: the A101, the B101, and the C101. Maxon allocates manufacturing overhead to each model based on machine hours. A large portion of the company's manufacturing overhead costs is incurred by the Maintenance Department. This year, the department anticipates that it will incur $80,000 in total costs. The following estimates pertain to the upcoming year:

Model	Estimated Machine Hours	Estimated Units of Production
A101	30,000	6,000
B101	15,000	4,000
C101	5,000	2,000

Jane Aire, Mason's cost accountant, suspects that unit costs are being distorted by using a single activity base to allocate Maintenance Department costs to products. Thus she is considering the implementation of activity-based costing (ABC).

Under the proposed ABC method, the costs of the Maintenance Department would be allocated to the following activity cost pools using the number of work orders as an activity base: (1) the repairs pool and (2) the janitorial pool. Of the 1,000 work orders filed with the Maintenance Department each year, approximately 200 relate to repair activities, and 800 relate to janitorial activities.

Machinery repairs correlate with the number of production runs of each robot model. Thus the repairs pool would be allocated to robots based on each model's corresponding number of production runs. Janitorial services correlate with square feet of production space. Thus the janitorial pool would be allocated to products based on the square feet of production space devoted to each robot model. The following table provides a summary of annual production run activity and square footage requirements:

Model	Estimated Number of Production Runs	Estimated Square Feet of Production Space Used
A101	40	10,000
B101	110	15,000
C101	150	25,000

Instructions

a. Calculate the amount of Maintenance Department costs that would be allocated to each robot model (on a per-unit basis) using machine hours as an activity base.
b. Calculate the amount of Maintenance Department costs that would be allocated to each robot model (on a per-unit basis) using the proposed ABC method.
c. Are cost allocations distorted using machine hours as a single activity base? Explain your answer.

CHAPTER 18 ALTERNATE PROBLEMS

Problem 18.1A
Identifying Value-Added and Non-Value-Added Activities

Smit Corporation is considering implementation of a JIT inventory system. The company's industrial engineer recently concluded a study to determine the average number of days spent in each activity of the production process. The following table summarizes her findings:

Production Activity	Number of Days
Inspection materials	6
Storing materials	35
Moving materials into production	5
Setting up production equipment	4
Cutting materials	13
Bending materials	10
Assembling finished products	19
Painting finished products	8

Instructions
  a. Identify Smit's value-added production activities.
  b. Identify Smit's non-value-added production activities.
  c. Calculate Smit's total cycle time.
  d. Determine Smit's manufacturing efficiency ratio.
  e. Which of the above activities might be reduced or eliminated if Smit implemented a JIT system?
  f. What ethical issues might be related to eliminating some of the non-value-added activities?

Problem 18.2A
Activity-Based Management and Target Costing

The Parvee Company manufactures two products: PAR, which sells for $100; and VEE, which sells for $200. Estimated cost and production data for the current year are as follows:

	PAR	VEE
Direct materials cost	$25	$40
Direct labor cost (@ $10/hr)	20	50
Estiimated production (units)	30,000	10,000

In addition, fixed manufacturing overhead is estimated to be $2,500,000 and variable overhead is estimated to equal $2.50 per direct labor hour. Parvee desires a 16% return on sales for all of its products.

Instructions
a. Calculate the target cost for both PAR and VEE.
b. Estimate the total manufacturing cost per unit of each product if fixed overhead costs are assigned to products on the basis of estimated production in units. Which of the products is earning the desired return?
c. Recalculate the total manufacturing cost per unit if fixed overhead costs are assigned to products on the basis of direct labor hours. Which of the products is earning the desired return? (Round to the nearest penny.)
d. Based on the confusing results of parts **b** and **c**, Parvee's manager decides to perform an activity analysis of fixed overhead. The results of the analysis are as follows:

			Demands	
Activity	Costs	Driver	PAR	VEE
Machine setups	$ 350,000	# of setups	100	300
Purchase orders	650,000	# of orders	300	100
Machining	500,000	# of machine-hours	3,000	4,000
Inspection	300,000	# of batches	40	20
Shipping to customers	200,000	# of shipments	400	100
Total fixed overhead	$2,000,000			

Estimate the total manufacturing cost per unit of each product if activity-based costing is used for assigning fixed overhead costs. Under this method, which product is earning the desired return?

e. What proportion of fixed overhead is value-added? In attempting to reach the target cost for VEE, which activity would you look to improving first and why?

Problem 18.3A
Target Costing

Oro Mining, Inc., has just discovered two new mining sites for copper. Geologists and engineers have come up with the following estimates regarding costs and copper yields if the mines are opened:

	Site A	Site Z
Variable extraction costs per ton............................	$4.20	$4.50
Fixed costs over the life of the mine:		
Blasting	$160,000	$200,000
Construction..	240,000	260,000
Maintenance..	30,000	30,000
Restoration costs	50,000	10,000
Total fixed costs...	$480,000	$500,000
Total tons of ore that can be extracted over the life of the mine:	240,000	200,000

Oro's owners currently demand a return of 18% of the market price of copper.

Instructions
a. If the current market price of copper is $10 per ton, what is Oro's target cost per ton?
b. Given the $10 market price, should either of the mines be opened?
c. The engineer working on Site Z believes that if a custom conveyer system is installed, the variable extraction cost could be reduced to $3.50 per ton. The purchase price of the system is $20,000, but the costs to restore the site will increase to $30,000 if it is installed. Given the current $10 market price, should Oro install the conveyer and open Site Z?

Problem 18.4A
Cost of Quality

Nazu, Inc., produces a popular brand of humidifiers that is backed by a five-year warranty. In the year 2001. Nazu began implementing a total quality management program that has resulted in significant changes in its cost of quality. Listed below is Nazu's financial information relating to sales and quality for the past two years.

	2001	2002
Sales revenue	$600,000	$600,000
Warranty expense	25,000	23,000
Product design	4,000	16,000
Scrap	3,000	1,000
Process reengineering	7,000	15,000
Raw materials inspections	5,200	2,000
Product liability claims	6,200	7,000
Rework	3,000	2,800
Returns resulting from defects	6,400	5,000
Supplier certification costs	600	2,000
Preventive maintenance on equipment	1,200	2,000
Final inspection costs	12,000	8,000
Employee quality training	1,400	3,000
Equipment breakdown repair costs	9,000	6,000
Estimate of lost sales due to quality problems	12,000	12,000

Instructions

a. Prepare a cost of quality report for Nazu covering the years 2001 and 2002. Your report should divide the above costs into the four categories of quality costs and include total dollar amounts for each category.

b. How have the total amounts of prevention and external failure costs changed over the two years? What are some possible explanations for these changes?

c. At Nazu, preventive maintenance has a direct effect on the repair costs associated with equipment breakdowns. Did the decrease in repair costs justify the increase in maintenance costs?

d. Why might Nazu's estimate of lost sales remain the same despire the adoption of the total quality management program?

CHAPTER 19 ALTERNATE PROBLEMS

Problem 19.1A
Using Cost-Volume Profit Formulas

Jumble writes and manufactures spelling games that it sells to retail stores. The following is per-unit information relating to the manufacture and sale of this product:

Unit sale price	$ 30
Variable cost per unit	6
Fixed costs per year	280,000

Instructions
Determine the following, showing as part of your answer the formula that you used in your computation. For example, the formula used to determine the contribution margin ratio (part **a**) is:

$$\text{Contribution Margin Ratio} = \frac{\text{Unit Sales Price} - \text{Variable Costs per Unit}}{\text{Unit Sales Price}}$$

a. Contribution margin ratio.
b. Sales volume (in dollars) required to break even.
c. Sales volume (in dollars) required to earn an annual operating income of $50,000.
d. The margin of safety sales volume if annual sales total 50,000 units.
e. Operating income if annual sales total 50,000 units.

Problem 19.2A
Using Cost-Volume-Profit Formulas

Spear Products typically earns a contribution margin ration on 30% and has current fixed costs of $90,000. Spear's general manager is considering spending an additional $25,000 to do one of the following:
1. Start a new ad campaign that is expected to increase sales revenue by 8%.
2. License a new computerized ordering system that is expected to increase Arrow's contribution margin ratio to 35%.

Sales revenue for the coming year was initially forecast to equal $1,500,000 (that is, without implementing either of the above options).

Instructions
- a. For each option, how much will projected operating income increase or decrease relative to initial predictions?
- b. By what percentage would sales revenue need to increase to make the ad campaign as attractive as the ordering system?

Problem 19.3A
Setting Sales Price and Computing the Break-Even Point

Barnie, Inc. is a newly organized manufacturing business that plans to manufacture and sell 100,000 units per year of a new product. The following estimates have been made of the company's costs and expenses (other than income taxes):

	Fixed	Variable per Unit
Manufacturing costs:		
Direct materials		$50
Direct labor		40
Manufacturing overhead	$ 600,000	10
Period expenses:		
Selling expenses		25
Administrative expenses	400,000	
Totals	$1,000,000	$125

Instructions

a. What should the company establish as the sales price per unit if it sets a target of earning an operating income of $400,000 by producing and selling 100,000 units during the first year of operations? (Hint: First compute the required contribution margin per unit.)

b. At the unit sales price computed in part **a**, how many units must the company produce and sell to break even? (Assume all units produced are sold.)

c. What will be the margin of safety (in dollars) if the company produces and sells 100,000 units at the sales price computed in part **a**? Using the margin of safety, compute operating income at 100,000 units.

d. Assume that the marketing manager thinks that the price of this product must be no higher than $130 to ensure market penetration. Will the setting the sales price at $130 enable Thermal Tent to break even, given the plans to manufacture and sell 150,000 units? Explain your answer.

Problem 19.4A
Estimating Costs and Profits

Swan Corporation manufactures ballet shoes. For the coming year, the company has budgeted the following costs for the production and sale of 50,000 pairs of shoes.

	Budgeted Costs	Budgeted Costs per Pair	Percentage of Costs Considered Variable
Direct materials	$ 750,000	$15	100%
Direct labor	250,000	5	100
Manufacturing overhead (fixed and variable)	600,000	12	30
Selling and administrative expenses	500,000	10	25
Totals	$2,100,000	$42	

Instructions

a. Compute the sales price per unit that would result in a budgeted operating income of $800,000 assuming that the company produces and sells 50,000 pairs. (Hint: First compute the budgeted sales revenue needed to produce this operating income.)

b. Assuming that the company decides to sell the shoes at a unit price of $100 per pair, compute the following:
  1. Total fixed costs budgeted for the year.
  2. Variable costs per unit.
  3. The unit contribution margin.
  4. The number of pairs that must be produced and sold annually to break even at a sales price of $100 per pair.

Problem 19.5A
Preparing a "Break-Even" Graph

Stay-a-While operates an uptown parking lot containing 1,000 parking spaces. The lot is open 5,000 hours per year. The parking charge per year is $1 per hour; the average customer parks two hours. Stay-a-While rents the lot for $6,000 per month. The lot supervisor is paid $25,000 per year. Six employees who handle the parking of cars are paid $400 per week for 50 weeks, plus $800 each for the two-week vacation period. Employees rotate vacations during the slow months when four employees can handle the reduced load of traffic. Lot maintenance, payroll taxes, and other costs of operating the parking lot include fixed costs of $2,000 per month and variable costs of 4 cents per parking-space hour.

Instructions
a. Draw a cost-volume-profit graph for Stay-a-While on an annual basis. Use thousands of parking-space hours as the measure of volume of activity. [Stay-a-While has an annual capacity of 5 million parking-space hours (1,000 spaces x 5,000 hours per year).]
b. What is the contribution margin ratio? What is the annual break-even point in dollars of parking revenue?
c. Suppose that the six employees were taken off the hourly wage basis and paid 40 cents per car parked, with the same vacation pay as before. (1) How would this change the contribution margin ratio and total fixed costs? (Hint: The variable costs per parking-space hour will now include 20 cents, or one-half of the 40 cents paid to employees per car parked, because the average customer parks for two hours.) (2) What annual sales revenue would be necessary to produce operating income of $200,000 under these circumstances?

Problem 19.6A
Drawing a Cost-Volume-Profit Graph

Hard Tiles operates a chain of tile stores. Although the tiles are sold under the Hard Tires label, it is purchased from an independent tile manufacturer. Gal Runner, president of Hard Tires, is studying the advisability of opening another store. Her estimates of monthly costs for the proposed location are:

Fixed costs:	
Occupancy costs..	$4,200
Salaries...	3,000
Other	1,500
Variable costs (including cost of tiles)...........	$8 per box

Although Hard Tiles stores sell several different types of tiles, monthly sales revenue consistently average $12 per box sold.

Instructions
a. Compute the contribution margin ratio and the break-even point in dollar sales and in boxes sold for the proposed store.
b. Draw a monthly cost-volume-profit graph for the proposed store, assuming 3,000 boxes per month as the maximum sales potential.
c. Runner thinks that the proposed store will sell between 2,500 and 3,000 boxes of the tiles per month. Compute the amount of operating income that would be earned per month at each of these sales volumes.

Problem 19.7A
Understanding Break-Even Relationships

Measure Up manufactures rules, which sells for $2.50 per unit. Management recently finished analyzing the results of the company's operations for the current month. At a break-even point of 30,000 units, the company's total variable costs are $60,000 and its total fixed costs amount to $40,000.

Instructions
- a. Calculate the contribution margin per unit.
- b. Calculate the company's margin of safety if monthly sales total 40,000 units.
- c. Estimate the company's monthly operating loss if it sells only 28,000 units.
- d. Compute the total cost per unit at a production level of (1) 30,000 pens per month and (2) 40,000 rulers per month. Explain the reason for the change in unit costs.

Problem 19.8A
Cost-Volume-Profit Analysis Preparing a Graph

Chez Giva is considering investing in a soda machine operation involving 20 soda machines located in various locations around the city. The machine manufacturer reports that similar soda machine routes have produced a sales volume ranging from 1,000 to 1,200 units per machine per month. The following information is made available to Giva in evaluating the possible profitability of the operation.

1. An investment of $50,000 will be required, $10,000 for merchandise and $40,000 for the 25 machines.
2. The machines have a service life of five years and no salvage value at the end of that period. Depreciation will be computed on the straight-line basis.
3. The merchandise (soft drinks) retails for an average of $1 per unit and will cost Giva an average of 40 cents per unit.
4. Owners of the buildings in which the machines are located are paid a commission of 5 cents per soft drinks sold.
5. One person will be hired to service the machines. The salary will be $1,200 per month.
6. Other expenses are estimated at $500 per month. These expenses do not vary with the number of units sold.

Instructions
a. Determine the unit contribution margin and the break-even volume in units and in dollars per month.
b. Draw a monthly cost-volume-profit graph for sales volume up to 1,000 units per machine per month.
c. What sales volume in units and in dollars per month will be necessary to produce an operating income equal to a 25% annual return on Giva's $50,000 investment? (Round to the nearest unit.)
d. Giva is considering offering the building owners a flat rental of $40 per machine per month in lieu of the commission of 5 cents per unit sold. What effect would this change in commission arrangement have on his *monthly* break-even volume in terms of units?

Problem 19.9A
Analyzing the Effects of Changes in Costs

Clip, Inc. manufactures staplers and currently sells 20,000 units annually. Sue Barnes, president of the company, anticipates a 10% increase in the cost per unit of direct labor on January 1 of next year. She expects all other costs and expenses to remain unchanged. Barnes has asked you to assist her in developing the information she needs to formulate a reasonable product strategy for the next year.

You are satisfied that volume is the primary factor affecting costs and expenses and have separated the semivariable costs into their fixed and variable segments. Beginning and ending inventories remain at a level of 800 units.

Below are the current-year data assembled for your analysis:

Sales price per unit...		$ 20
Variable costs per unit:		
Direct materials..	$4	
Direct labor	5	
Manufacturing overhead and selling		
and administrative expenses	5	14
Contribution margin per unit 30%...........................		$ 6
Fixed costs		$200,000

Instructions

a. What increase in the selling price is necessary to cover the 10% increase in direct labor cost and still maintain the current contribution margin ratio of 30%?

b. How many staplers must be sold to maintain the current operating income of $260,000 if the sales price remains at $20 and the 10% wage increase goes into effect? (Hint: First compute the unit contribution margin.)

c. Barnes believes that an additional $500,000 of machinery (to be depreciated at 20% annually) will increase present capacity (100,000 units) by 25%. If all staplers produced can be sold at the present price of $20 per unit and the wage increase goes into effect, how would the estimated operating income before capacity is increased compare with the estimated operating income after capacity is increased? Prepare schedules of estimated operating income at full capacity *before* and *after* the expansion.

Problem 19.10A
Analyzing the Effects of Changes in Costs and Volumes

Outel, Inc. produces two versions of its popular Digel processors. For the coming year, fixed manufacturing costs are projected to equal $160,000. Information regarding forecast unit selling prices, variable costs, and demand for each processor is as follows:

	Unit Selling Price	Unit Variable Manufacturing Costs	Units Demanded
Apple	$120	$ 50	$6,000
Pear	600	120	1,500

Instructions

Suppose Outel must choose only one of the processors to manufacture. Analyze the following scenarios:

a. Based on the above prices, costs, and demand, which processor will result in the highest operating income?

b. Outel's marketing managers project that if the selling price of the Digel processor is reduced by 25%, demand will double. Likewise, if the selling price of the Pear is reduced by 60%, demand will triple. Will adopting either of these alternative pricing strategies result in greater operating income than that found in part **a** (assuming no changes in manufacturing costs)?

c. Outel has an opportunity to adopt a new manufacturing process that will increase its fixed costs to $280,000. The new process will reduce the variable manufacturing cots of the Apple processor should be manufactured and at which of the two suggested prices should it be sold to earn the highest operating income? Should the process be adopted?

d. What overall strategy combination (that is, original versus new process, Apple versus Pear, original versus alternative selling price) should be chosen to maximize expected operating income? If your answer is different than in part **a**, explain why it results in a greater level of operating income.

Problem 19.11A
Analyzing the Effects of Changes in Costs and Volumes

Charlie Farms raises marine fish for sale in the aquarium trade. Each year, Charlie obtains a batch of approximately 1 million eggs from a local supplier. Charlie's manager is trying to decide whether to use the farm's facilities to raise dogfish or catfish. Dogfish eggs cost $6,000 per batch, while catfish eggs cost $10,000 per batch. Due to differences in needs, only one species may be raised at a time and only one batch of fish can be raised in any 52-week period.

With current facilities, approximately 12% of dogfish eggs and 6% of catfish eggs can be successfully raised to maturity. Dogfish take approximately 40 weeks to grow to a saleable size, while catfish take 50 weeks. Catfish also require more care than dogfish. Each week, catfish need two complete water changes and 20 feedings, while dogfish need only one water change and 15 feedings. Each feeding costs $160 and each water change costs $800. Heating and lighting costs equal $300 per week of rearing, regardless of which fish and being raised. Fixed overhead costs for the year amount to $100,000. Charlie can sell dogfish for $5 each and catfish for $12 each.

Instructions
a. Which species should Charlie raise to earn the highest operating income for the year?
b. Other than fixed costs, which factors or categories of costs seem to have the greatest influence on operating income?
c. Charlie's manager is considering the following improvements, each of which will cost an additional $10,000 for the year. Due to resource limitations, only one can be implemented.
  1. Purchasing a higher quality filter material that will significantly improve water conditions in the rearing tanks. The higher water quality will increase the survival rates to 14% for dogfish and 8% for catfish. The need for water changes will also be reduced to one each week for both species of fish. Due to the higher yields, feeding costs will increase to $160 each.
  2. Installing newer, more efficient equipment that will reduce heating and lighting costs to $200 per week of rearing. The new equipment will promote more stable conditions, increasing the survival rates of dogfish to 12.5% and of catfish to 6.5%. The slight change in survival rates is not expected to increase feeding costs.

  Using your answers to part **b** above (with no calculations), which options do you think will be more beneficial?
d. Perform the necessary calculations to check if your answer to part **c** was correct. Should either of the investments be undertaken, and if so, which fish species should be raised?

Problem 19.12A
CVP with Multiple Products

B-Ball, Inc. sells gloves and bats. The following is selected per-unit information for these two products:

	Gloves	Bats
Sales price	$60	$8
Variable costs and expenses	40	2
Contribution margin	$20	$6

Fixed costs and expenses amount to $400,000 per month.
    B-Ball has total sales of $1,500,000 million per month, of which 75% results from the sale of running gloves and the other 25% from sales of bats.

Instructions
- **a.** Compute separately the contribution margin ratio for each line of products.
- **b.** Assuming the current sales mix, compute:
    1. Average contribution margin ratio of total monthly sales.
    2. Monthly operating income.
    3. The monthly break-even sales volume (stated in, dollars).
- **c.** Assume that through aggressive marketing, B-Ball is able to *shift its sales mix* toward move sales of bats. Total sales remain $1,500,000 per month, but now 30% of this revenue stems from sales of bats. Using this new sales mix, compute:
    1. Average contribution margin ratio of total monthly sales.
    2. Monthly operating income.
    3. The monthly break-even sales volume (stated in dollars).
- **d.** Explain *why* the company's financial picture changes so significantly with the new sales mix.

CHAPTER 20 ALTERNATE PROBLEMS

Problem 20.1A
Evaluating a Special Order

F. Scott designs and manufactures fashionable women's clothing. For the coming year, the company has scheduled production of 50,000 silk skirts. Budgeted costs for this product are as follows:

	Unit Costs (50,000 Units)	Total
Variable manufacturing costs	$40	$2,000,000
Variable selling expenses	15	750,000
Fixed manufacturing costs	12	600,000
Fixed operating expenses	10	500,000
Total costs and expenses	$77	$3,850,000

The management of F. Scott is considering a special order from Discount Fashions for an additional 15,000 skirts. These skirts would carry the Discount Fashions label, rather than the F. Scott label. In all other respects, they would be identical to the regular F. Scott jackets.

Although F. Scott regularly sells its skirts to retail stores at a price of $180 each, Discount Fashions has offered to pay only $60 per skirt. However, because no sales commissions would be involved with this special order, F. Scott will incur variable selling expenses of only $5 per unit on these sales, rather than the $15 it normally incurs. Accepting the order would cause no change in the company's fixed manufacturing costs or fixed operating costs. F. Scott has enough plant capacity to produce 70,000 skirts per year.

Instructions
a. Using incremental revenue and incremental costs, compute the expected effect of accepting this special order on F. Scott's operating income.
b. Briefly discuss any other factors that you believe F. Scott's management should consider in deciding whether to accept the special order. Include nonfinancial as well as financial considerations.

Problem 20.2A
Evaluating a Special Order

The Formost Company sells 800,000 units per year of a particular software program at $20 each. The current unit cost of the program is broken down as follows:

Direct materials	$ 5.00
Direct labor	2.00
Variable factory overhead	1.00
Fixed factory overhead	3.00
Total	$11.00

At the beginning of the current year, Formost received a special order for 20,000 of these programs per month *for one year only*, at a sales price of $9 per unit. To fill the order, Formost will have to rent additional assembly space at a cost of $15,000 ($1,250 per month).

Instructions
Compute the estimated increase or decrease in annual operating income that will result from accepting this special offer.

Problem 20.3A
Make or Buy Decision

Matchless Corp. manufactures radios that it uses in several of its products. Management is considering whether to continue manufacturing the radios or to buy them from an outside source. The following information is available:
1. The company needs 20,000 radios per year. The radios can be purchased from an outside supplier at a cost of $50 per unit.
2. The unit cost of manufacturing the radios is $85 computed as follows:

Direct materials...	$ 400,000
Direct labor	500,000
Factory overhead:	
Variable..	350,000
Fixed	450,000
Total manufacturing costs...	$1,700,000
Cost per unit ($1,700,000 ÷ 20,000)..	$85

3. Discontinuing the manufacture of radios will eliminate all the raw materials and direct labor costs but will eliminate only 80% of the variable factory overhead costs.
4. If the radios are purchased from an outside source, machinery used in the production of radios will be sold at its book value. Accordingly, no gain or loss will be recognized. The sale of this machinery would also eliminate $5,000 in fixed costs associated with depreciation and taxes. No other reductions in fixed factory overhead will result from discontinuing the production of radios.

Instructions
a. Prepare a schedule in the format illustrated in Chapter 20 of the text to determine the incremental cost or benefit of buying the radios from the outside supplier. Based on this schedule, would you recommend that the company manufacture the radios or buy them from the outside source?
b. Assume that if the radios are purchased from the outside source, the factory space previously used to produce radios can be used to manufacture an additional 8,000 timepieces per year. Timepieces have an estimated contribution margin of $15 per unit. The manufacture of the additional timepieces would have no effect on fixed factory overhead. Would this new assumption change your recommendation as to whether to make or buy the radios? In support of your conclusion, prepare a schedule showing the incremental cost or benefit of buying the radios from the outside source and using the factory space to production additional timepieces.

Problem 20.4A
Make or Buy Decision

James Lighting manufactures switches that it uses in several of its products. Management is considering whether to continue manufacturing the switches or to buy them from an outside source. The following information is available:

1. The company needs 100,000 switches per year. Switches can be purchased from an outside supplier at a cost of $4 per unit.
2. The cost of manufacturing switches is $5.00 per unit, computed as follows:

Direct materials	$ 150,000
Direct labor	100,000
Manufacturing overhead:	
Variable	200,000
Fixed	50,000
Total manufacturing costs	$ 500,000
Cost per unit ($500,000 ÷ 100,000)	$5.00

3. Discontinuing the manufacture of the switches will eliminate all of the direct materials and direct labor costs but will eliminate only 70% of the variable overhead costs.
4. If the switches are purchased from an outside source, certain machinery used in the production process would no longer have to be leased. Accordingly, $19,000 of fixed overhead costs could be avoided. No other reduction will result from discontinuing production of the switches.

Instructions

a. Prepare a schedule to determine the incremental cost or benefit of buying switches from the outside supplier. Based on this schedule, would you recommend that the company manufacture the switches or buy them from the outside source?
b. Assume that if switches are purchased from the outside source, the factory space previously used to produce switches can be used to manufacture an additional 10,000 whosas per year. These whosas have an estimated contribution margin of $14 per unit. The manufacture of the additional whosas would have no effect on fixed overhead. Would this new assumption change your recommendation as to whether to make or buy switches? In support of your conclusion, prepare a schedule showing the incremental cost or benefit of buying switches from the outside source and using the factory space to production additional whosas.

Problem 20.5A
Determining the Most Profitable Product Given Scarce Resources

Superior Instruments produces two models of instruments. Information for each model is as follows:

	Model A	Model B
Sales price per unit...	$300	$155
Costs and expenses per unit:		
Direct materials..	$60	$50
Direct labor	40	20
Manufacturing overhead (applied at the rate of $24 per machine-hour, 1/3 of which is fixed and 2/3 variable)..	72	24
Variable selling expenses..	62	24
Total costs and expenses per unit............................	234	111
Profit per unit...	$ 66	$ 39
Machine-hours required to produce one unit..............	3	1

The demand for either product is sufficient to keep the plant operating at full capacity of 15,000 machine-hours per month. Assume that *only one product is to be produced in the future.*

Instructions
a. Prepare a schedule showing the contribution margin per machine-hour for each product.
b. Explain your recommendation as to which of the two products should be discontinued.

Problem 20.6A
Scarce Resources

Home Run Corporation produces three products for baseball enthusiasts: bats, gloves, and balls. Information relating to each product line is as follows:

	Bats	Gloves	Balls
Selling price	$48	$80	$12
Direct materials	14	10	1
Direct labor	8	24	4
Variable overhead	1	1	1

Home Run pays its direct labor workers an average of $8 per hour. At full capacity, 60,000 direct labor hours are available per year. The marketing department has just released the following sales estimates for the upcoming year: bats (60,000 units), gloves (20,000 units), balls (100,000 units). Based on these figures, demand for the current year is expected to exceed the company's direct labor capacity.

Instructions
a. What products should Home Run produce to maximize its operating income?
b. The company's marketing manager believes that the production of the lease profitable product is needed to "support" the demand for the most profitable products. How may this influence management's decision regarding the company's production schedule?

Problem 20.7A
Sell or Rebuild Deficient Units

Bold Face manufactures TV's. The company's color TV's are very popular, but it has an inventory of 500 large screen, black and white TV's for which there is little demand. Bold Face is considering the following options for disposing of these TV's:
1. Sell them to a discount mail-order company at a total price of $40,000. The mail-order firm would then sell these large screen TV's at a unit price of $200.
2. Convert them to color TV's at a remanufacturing cost of $400 per unit. These TV's then could be sold to TV stores for $1,000 each.

The black and white TV's had been manufactured at a cost of $300 per unit. The cost of manufacturing color TV's of the same size, however, normally amounts to $410 per unit.

Instructions
a. Perform an incremental analysis of the revenue, costs, and gross profit resulting from converting the black and white TV's to color as compared with selling them to the mail-order firm.
b. Identify any sunk costs, out-of-pocket costs, and possible opportunity costs.
c. Indicate which of these options you would select and explain your reasoning, assuming that Bold Face currently:
   1. Has substantial excess capacity.
   2. Is operating at full capacity manufacturing color TV's.

Problem 20.8A
Sell of Rebuild

Fire Code manufactures smoke detectors that are sold to homeowners throughout the United States at $20 a piece. Each detector is equipped with a sensory cell that is guaranteed to last two full years before needing to be replaced. The company currently has 80,000 smoke detectors in its inventory that contains sensory cells that had been purchased from a discount vendor. Fire Code engineers estimate that these sensory cells will last only 18 months before needing to be replaced. The company has incurred the following unit costs related to the 80,000 detectors:

Direct materials	$ 8
Direct labor	1
Variable overhead	2
Fixed overhead	1
Total	$12

Fire Code is currently evaluating three options regarding the 80,000 detectors:
1. Scrap the inferior sensory cell in each unit and replace it with a new one at a cost of $6 each. The units could then be sold at their full unit price of $20.
2. Sell the units with the inferior sensory cells at a discounted unit price of $18. This option would also involve changing the packaging of each unit to inform the buyer that the estimated life of the sensory cell is 18 months. The estimated out-of-pocket cost associated with the packaging changes is $2 per unit.
3. Sell each unit "as is" with its current packaging to a discount buyer in a foreign country. The buyer has offered to pay Fire Code a unit price of $17.

Instructions
a. Perform the incremental analysis of these options. Based on the analysis, which option should Fire Code choose?
b. What nonfinancial concerns should the company take into consideration?

Problem 20.9A
Joint Products

Green Leaf produces three joint products from seaweed. At the split-off point, three basic products emerge: Sea Tea, Sea Paste, and Sea Powder. Each of these products can either be sold at the split-off point or be processed further. If they are processed further, the resulting products can be sold as delicacies to health food stores. Cost and revenue information is as follows:

Product	Pounds Produced	Sales Value at Split-Off	Final Sales Value	Additional Cost
Sea Tea	$10,000	$ 80,000	$100,000	$30,000
Sea Paste	5,000	100,000	180,000	60,000
Sea Powder	3,000	90,000	110,000	10,000

Sales Value and Additional Costs if Process Further

Instruction
- a. Which products should Green Leaf process beyond the split-off point?
- b. At what price per pound would it be advantageous for Green Leaf Company to sell Sea Paste at the split-off point rather than process it further?

CHAPTER 21 ALTERNATE PROBLEMS

Problem 21.1A
Types of Responsibility Centers and Basis for Evaluation

Listed below are parts of various well-known businesses:
1. The bookstore of Northern Jersey University.
2. The billing department of Rhode Island Life Insurance Co.
3. The Norwalk Factory of Melvin's Chocolates.
4. The jewelry department of Bloomingdale's.
5. The gift shop at the Museum of Natural History.
6. The legal department of Sears.

Instructions
a. Indicate whether each part represents an investment center, a profit center (other than an investment center), or a cost center.
b. Briefly explain the criteria that are used in evaluating (1) investment centers, (2) profit center, and (3) cost centers.

Problem 21.2A
Preparing and Using Responsibility Income Statements

Brown Enterprises has two product lines: bags and shoes. Cost and revenue data for each product line for the current month are as follows:

	Product Lines	
	Bags	**Shoes**
Sales...	$1,000,000	$500,000
Variable costs as a percentage of sales.......................	60%	30%
Fixed costs traceable to product lines........................	$250,000	$275,000

In addition to the costs shown above, the company incurs monthly fixed costs of $75,000 common to both product lines.

Instructions
a. Prepare Brown Enterprises' responsibility income statement for the current month. Report the responsibility margin for each product line and income from operations for the company as a whole. Also include columns showing all dollar amounts as percentages of sales.
b. Assume that a marketing survey shows that a $50,000 monthly advertising campaign focused on either product line should increase that product line's monthly sales by approximately $100,000. Do you recommend this additional advertising for either or both product lines? Show computations to support your conclusions.
c. Management is considering expanding one of the company's two product lines. An investment of a given dollar amount is expected to increase the sales of the expanded product line by $250,000. It is also expected to increase the traceable fixed costs of the expanded product line by 60%. Based on this information, which product line do you recommend expanding? Explain the basis for your conclusions.

Problem 21.3A
Preparing and Using a Responsibility Income Statement

The Robinns Company is organized into two divisions: Deluxe and Standard. During August, sales for the Deluxe Division totaled $2,000,0000, and its contribution margin ratio averaged 35%. Sales generated by the Standard Division totaled $1,200,000 and its contribution margin ratio averaged 50%. Monthly fixed costs traceable to each division total $200,000. Common fixed costs for the month amount to $100,000.

Instructions
a. Prepare Robinns Company's responsibility income statement for the current month. Be certain to report responsibility margin for each division and income from operations for the company as a whole. Also include columns showing all dollar amounts as percentages of sales.
b. Compute the dollar sales volume required for the Standard Division to earn a monthly responsibility margin of $600,000.
c. A marketing study indicates that sales in the Standard Division would increase by 4% if advertising expenditures for the division were increased by $12,000 per month. Would you recommend this increase in advertising? Show computations to support your decision.

Problem 21.4A
Preparing Responsibility Income Statement in a Responsibility Accounting System

Freeze, Inc. sells air conditioners. The company has two sales territories, Northern and Southern. Two products are sold in each territory: Economy and Efficiency.

During January, the following data are reported for the Northern territory:

	Economy	Efficiency
Sales	$500,000	$1,000,000
Contribution margin ratios	70%	30%
Traceable fixed costs	$ 90,000	$ 200,000

Common fixed costs in the Northern territory amounted to $125,000 during the month.

During January, the Southern territory reported total sales of $800,000, variable costs of $352,000, and a responsibility margin of $250,000. Freeze also incurred $140,000 of common fixed costs that were not traceable to either sales territory.

In addition to being profit centers, each territory is also evaluated as an investment center. Average assets utilized by the Northern and Southern territories amount to $16,000,000 and $10,000,000 respectively.

Instructions

a. Prepare the January income statement for the Northern territory by product line. Include columns showing percentages as well as dollar amounts.
b. Prepare the January income statement for the company showing profits by sales territories. Conclude your statement with income from operations for the company and with responsibility margins for the two territories. Show percentages as well as dollar amounts.
c. Compute the rate of return on average assets earned in each sales territory during the month of January.
d. If part **a**, your income statement for the Northern territory included $125,000 in common fixed costs. What happened to these common fixed costs in the responsibility income statements shown in part **b**?
e. The manager of the Northern territory is authorized to spend an additional $40,000 per month in advertising one of the products. Based on past experience, the manager estimates that additional advertising would increase the sales of either product by $100,000. On which product should the manager focus this advertising campaign? Explain.
f. Top management is considering investing several million dollars to expand operations in one of its two sales territories. The expansion would increase traceable fixed costs to expanded territory in proportion to its increase in sales. Which territory would be the best candidate for this investment? Explain.

Problem 21.5A
Analysis of Responsibility Income Statements

Shown below are responsibility income statements for Sotheby, Inc., for the month of June.

	\multicolumn{6}{c}{Investment Centers}
	\multicolumn{2}{c}{Sotheby Inc.}	\multicolumn{2}{c}{Division 1}	\multicolumn{2}{c}{Division 2}
	Dollars	%	Dollars	%	Dollars	%
Sales	$500,000	100	$340,000	100	$160,000	100
Variable costs	302,000	60	238,000	70	64,000	40
Contribution margin	198	40	102,000	30	96,000	60
Fixed costs traceable to divisions	132	26	68,000	20	64,000	40
Division responsibility margins	66	13	34,000	10	32,000	20
Common fixed costs	46	9				
Income from operations	20	4				

	\multicolumn{6}{c}{Profit Centers}
	\multicolumn{2}{c}{Division 1}	\multicolumn{2}{c}{Product C}	\multicolumn{2}{c}{Product D}
	Dollars	%	Dollars	%	Dollars	%
Sales	$340,000	100	$120,000	100	$220,000	100
Variable costs	238,000	70	60,000	50	178,000	81
Contribution margin	102,000	30	60,000	50	42,000	19
Fixed costs traceable to products	48,000	14	28,000	23	20,000	9
Product responsibility margins	54,000	16	32,000	27	22,000	10
Common fixed costs	20,000	6				
Responsibility margin for division	34,000	10				

Instructions

a. The company plans to initiate an advertising campaign for one of the two products in Division 1. The campaign would cost $8,000 per month and is expected to increase the sales of whichever product is advertised by $25,000 per month. Compute the expected increase in the responsibility margin of Division 1 assuming that (1) product C is advertised and (2) product D is advertised.

b. Assume that the sales of both products by Division 1 are equal to total manufacturing capacity. To increase sales of either product, the company must increase manufacturing facilities, which means an increase in traceable fixed costs in approximate proportion to the expected increase in sales. In this case, which product line would you recommend expanding? Explain.

c. The income statement for Division 1 includes $20,000 in common fixed costs. What happens to these fixed costs in the income statements for Sotheby, Inc.?
d. Assume that in November the monthly sales in Division 2 increase to $200,000. Compute the expected effect of this change on the operating income of the company (assume no other changes in revenue or cost behavior).
e. Prepare an income statement for Sotheby, Inc., by division, under the assumption stated In part **d**. Organize this income statement in the format illustrated above, including columns for percentages.

Problem 21.6A
Evaluating an Unprofitable Business Center

Foot B, inc. is a small manufacturer of professional football equipment. The company has two divisions: the Pad Division and the Helmet Division. Data for the month of June are as follows:

	Entire Company	Pad Division	Helmet Division
		Profit Centers	
Sales	$70,000	$30,0000	$40,000
Variable costs	30,000	15,000	15,000
Contribution margins	$40,000	$15,000	$25,000
Traceable fixed costs	30,000	18,000	12,000
Division responsibility margins	$10,000	$(3,000)	$13,000
Common fixed costs	4,000		
Monthly operating income	$ 6,000		

Jacques, the company's chief financial officer since June 1 of the current year, wants to close the unprofitable Pad Division. He believes that doing so will benefit Foot B and benefit him, given that his end-of-year bonus is to be based on the company's overall operating income. In a recent interview, Jacques summarized his business philosophy as follows: "A company is only as strong as its least profitable segment. As long as I'm at the financial helm, only the strongest shall survive at Foot B."

Instructions
a. Had the Pad Division been closed on *January 1*, what would the company's operating income for the month have been?
b. After learning about Jacque's business philosophy, the Pad Division's director of marketing made the following statement: "Jacques may understand numbers, but he doesn't understand the complementary relationship between pads and helmets, nor the seasonal nature of our business." What did the director of marketing mean by this statement? How might such information influence Jacque's assessment of the company's Pad Division?
c. By how much would the Pad Division's monthly sales have to increase for it to generate a positive responsibility margin of $2,000 in any given month? Show all your computations.

Problem 21.7A
Transfer Pricing Decisions

Eastrise Corporation has two divisions: the Motor Division and the Mower Division. The Motor Division supplies the motors used by the Mower Division. The Mower Division produces approximately 10,000 mowers annually. Thus it receives 10,000 motors from the Motor Division each year. The market price of these motors is $400. Their total variable cost is $220 per unit. The market price of the mower is $600. The unit variable cost of each mower, excluding the cost of the motor, is $100.

The Motor Division is currently operating at full capacity, producing 30,000 motors per year (10,000 of which are transferred to the Mower Division). The demand for the motors is so great that all 30,000 units could be sold to outside customers if the Mower Division acquired its motors elsewhere. The Motor Division uses the full market price of $400 as the transfer price charged to the Mower Division.

The manager of the Mower Division asserts that the Motor Division benefits from the inter-company transfers because of reduced advertising costs. Thus he wants to negotiate a lower transfer price of $380 per unit.

Instructions
a. Compute the contribution margin earned annually by each division and by the company as a whole using the current transfer price.
b. Compute the contribution margin that would be earned annually by each division by the company as a whole if the discounted transfer price were used.
c. What issues and concerns should be considered in setting a transfer price for intercompany transfers of motors?

Problem 21.8A
Variable Costing

Billgot Corporation manufactures and sells a single product. The following costs were incurred during 2002, the company's first year of operations:

Variable costs per unit:	
Direct materials..	$20
Direct labor	10
Variable manufacturing overhead...	4
Variable selling and administrative expenses.......................	8
Fixed costs for the year:	
Manufacturing overhead..	$1,000,000
Selling and administrative expenses....................................	200,000

During the year, the company manufactured 100,000 units, of which 80,000 were sold at a price of $80 per unit. The 20,000 units in inventory at year-end were all finished goods.

Instructions
a. Assuming that the company uses full costing:
   1. Determine the per-unit cost of each finished good manufactured during 2002.
   2. Prepare a partial income statement for the year, ending with income from operations.
b. Assuming that the company uses variable costing:
   1. Determine the per-unit cost of each finished good manufactured during 2002.
   2. Prepare a partial income statement for the year, ending with income from operations.
c. Explain why your income statements in parts **a** and **b** result in different amounts of income from operations. Indicate which costing approach is used in published financial statements, and briefly explain the usefulness of the other approach.
d. Using the data contained in the variable costing income statement, compute (1) the contribution margin per unit sold and (2) the unit sales volume that must be manufactured and sold annually for Billgot Corporation to break even.

CHAPTER 22 ALTERNATE PROBLEMS

Problem 22.1A
Budgeting Manufacturing Overhead

Wells Enterprises manufactures a component that is processed successively by Department I and Department II. Manufacturing overhead is applied to units produced at the following budget costs:

	Manufacturing Overhead per Unit		
	Fixed	Variable	Total
Department I	$15	$8	$20
Department II	12	6	15

These budgeted overhead costs per unit are based on a normal volume of production of 5,000 units per month. In January, variable manufacturing overhead in Department II is expected to be 20% above budget because of major scheduled repairs to equipment. The company plans to produce 8,000 units during January.

Instructions
Prepare a budget for manufacturing overhead costs in January. Use three column headings: Total, Department I, and Department II.

Problem 22.2A
Budgeting Labor Costs

Deep Valley Foods manufactures a product that is first smoked and then packed for shipment to customers. The product's direct labor cost per pound is budgeted using the following information:

	Direct Labor Hours per Pound	Budgeted Direct Labor Cost per Hour
Process:		
Smoking	.04	$10.00
Packing	.01	8.00

The budget for March calls for the production of 500,000 pounds of product. March's direct labor costs for smoking are expected to be 5% above budget due to anticipated scheduling inefficiencies. However, direct labor costs in the packing room are expected to be 3% below budget because of changes in equipment layout.

Instructions

Prepare a budget for direct labor costs in March. Use three column headings: Total, Smoking, and Packing.

Problem 22.3A
Budgeting Production, Inventories, and Cost of Sales

Frowren Domestic manufactures and sells a single product. In preparing its master budget for the current quarter, the company's controller has assembled the following information:

	Units	Dollars
Sales (budgeted)	200,000	$8,000,000
Finished goods inventory, beginning of quarter	30,000	750,000
Finished goods inventory, end of quarter	25,000	?
Cost of finished goods manufactured (assume a Budgeted manufacturing cost of $26 per unit)	?	?

Frowren Domestic used the average cost method of pricing its inventory of finished goods.

Instructions
Compute the following budgeted quantities or dollar amounts:
a. Planned production of finished goods (in units).
b. Cost of finished goods manufactured.
c. Ending finished goods inventory (Remember that in using the average cost method, you must first compute the average cost of units available for sale.)
d. Cost of goods sold.

Problem 22.4A
Short Budgeting Problem

Melody Corporation manufactures and sells a single product. In preparing the budget for the first quarter, the company's cost accountant has assembled the following information:

	Units	Dollars
Sales (budgeted)..	200,000	$15,000,000
Finished goods inventory, Jan. 1 (actual)....................	40,000	1,440,000
Finished goods inventory, Mar. 31 (budgeted)...........	30,000	?
Cost of finished goods manufactured (budgeted manufacturing cost is $38 per unit)	?	?

The company uses the first-in, first-out method of pricing its inventory of finished goods.

Instructions
Compute the following budgeted quantities or dollar amounts:
  a. Planned production of finished goods (in units).
  b. Cost of finished goods manufactured.
  c. Finished goods inventory, March 31 (Remember to use the first-in, first-out method in pricing the inventory.)
  d. Cost of goods sold.

Problem 22.5A
Budgeting for Cash

Baily Distributors wants a projection of cash receipts and cash payments for the month of November. On November 28, a note will be payable in the amount of $92,250, including interest. The cash balance on November 1 is $37,200. Accounts payable to merchandise creditors at the end of October were $206,000.

The company's experience indicates that 75% of sales will be collected during the month of sale, 20% in the month following the sale, and 3% in the second month following the sale; 2% will be uncollectible. The company sells various products at an average price of $10 per unit. Selected sales figures are as follows:

	Units
Sept. – actual	40,000
Oct. – actual	70,000
Nov. – estimated	90,000
Dec. – estimated	60,000
Total estimated for the current year	900,000

Because purchases are payable within 15 days, approximately 50% of the purchases in a given month are paid in the following month. The average cost of units purchased is $6 per unit. Inventories at the end of each month are maintained at a level of 2,000 units plus 10% of the number of units that will be sold in the following month. The inventory on October 1 amounted to 9,000 units.

Budgeted operating expenses for November are $250,000. Of this amount, $100,000 is considered fixed (including depreciation of $40,000). All operating expenses, other than depreciation, are paid in the month in which they are incurred.

The company expects to sell fully depreciated equipment in November for $9,000 cash.

Instructions
Prepare a cash budget for the month of November, supported by schedules of cash collections on accounts receivable and cash payments for purchases of merchandise.

Problem 22.6A
Estimating Borrowing Requirements

Peter Corporation sells its products to a single customer. At the beginning of the current quarter, the company reports the following selected account balances:

Cash..	$ 10,000
Accounts receivable..	250,000
Current payables	90,000

Peter's management has made the following budget estimates regarding operations for the current quarter.

Sales (estimated)...	$700,000
Total costs and expenses (estimated)...	500,000
Debt service payment (estimated)..	260,000
Tax liability payment (estimated)...	50,000

Of Peter's total costs and expenses, $40,000 is quarterly depreciation expense, and $18,000 represents the expiration of prepayments. The remaining $442,000 is to be financed with current payables. The company's ending prepayments balance is expected to be the same as its beginning prepayments balance. Its ending current payables balance is expected to be $15,000 more than its beginning balance.

All of Peter's sales are on account. Approximately 70% of its sales are collected in the quarter in which they are made. The remaining 30% is collected in the following quarter. Because all of the company's sales are made to a single customer, it experiences virtually no uncollectible accounts.

Peter's minimum cash balance requirement is $10,000. Should the balance fall below this amount, management negotiates a short-term loan with a local bank. The company's debt ratio (liabilities ÷ assets) is currently 90%.

Instructions
a. Compute Peter's budgeted cash receipts for the quarter.
b. Compute Peter's payments of current payables budgeted for the quarter.
c. Compute Peter's cash prepayments budgeted for the quarter.
d. Prepare Peter's cash budget for the quarter.
e. Estimate Peter's short-term borrowing requirement for the quarter.
f. Discuss problems Peter might encounter in obtaining short-term financing.

Problem 22.7A
Budgeted Income Statement and Cash Budget

Synder's has been in business since January of the current year. The company buys fresh pasta crusts and resells them to large supermarket chains in five states. The following information pertains for Synder's first four months of operations:

	Purchases	Sales
Jan.	$50,000	$80,000
Feb.	40,000	60,000
Mar.	55,000	90,000
Apr.	25,000	40,000

Synder's expects to open several new sales territories in May. In anticipation of increased volume, management forecasts May sales at $100,000. To meet this demand, purchases in May are budgeted at $60,000. The company maintains a gross profit margin of approximately 40%.

All of Synder's sales are on account. Due to strict credit policies, the company has no bad debt expense. The following collection performance is anticipated for the remainder of the year:

Percent collected in month of sale	40%
Percent collected in month following sale	50%
Percent collected in the second month following sale	10%

Synder's normally pays for 75% of its purchases in the month that the purchases are made. The remaining amount is paid in the following month. The company's fixed selling and administrative expenses average $10,000 per month. Of this amount, $3,000 is depreciation expense. Variable selling and administrative expenses in the month that they are incurred.

Synder's debt service is $4,000 per month. Of this amount, approximately $3,000 represents interest expense, and $1,000 is payment on the principal. The company's tax rate is approximately 25%. Quarterly tax payments are made at the end of March, June, September, and December.

Instructions
a. Prepare Synder's budgeted income statement for May.
b. Prepare Synder's cash budget for May. Assume that the company's cash balance on May 1 is $30,000.
c. Explain why Synder's budgeted cash flow in May differs from its budgeted net income.

Problem 22.8A
Preparing a Cash Budget

Jill Marlow, owner of Marlow Industries, is negotiating with the bank for a $250,000, 90-day, 15% loan effective July 1 of the current year. If the bank grants the loan, the net proceeds will be $240,000, which Marlow intends to use on July 1 as follows: pay accounts payable, $200,000; purchase equipment, $25,000; add to bank balance, $15,000.

The current working capital position of Marlow Industries, according to financial statements as of June 30 is as follows:

Cash in bank...	$ 18,000
Receivables (net of allowance for doubtful accounts)..............	200,000
Merchandise inventory...	80,000
Total current assets	$298,000
Accounts payable (including accrued operating expenses)	160,000
Working capital...	$138,000

The bank loan officer asks Marlow to prepare a forecast of her cash receipts and cash payments for the next three months to demonstrate that the loan can be repaid at the end of September.

Marlow has made the following estimates, which are to be used in preparing a three-month cash budget: Sales (all on account) for July, $320,000; August, $400,000; September, $280,000; and October, $210,000. Past experience indicates that 75% of the receivables generated in any month following the sale, and 1% will prove uncollectible. Marlow expects to collect $160,000 of the June 30 receivables in July and the remaining $40,000 in August.

Cost of goods sold consistently has averaged about 65% of sales. Operating expenses are budgeted at $40,000 per month plus 10% of sales. With the exception of $5,000 per month depreciation expense, all operating expenses and purchases are on account and are paid in the month following their incurrence.

Merchandise inventory at the end of each month should be sufficient to cover the following month's sales.

Instructions
a. Prepare a monthly cash budget showing estimated cash receipts and cash payments for July, August, and September, and the cash balance at the end of each month. Supporting schedules should be prepared for estimated collections on receivables, estimated merchandise purchases, and estimated payments for operating expenses and of accounts payable for merchandise purchases.
b. On the basis of this cash forecast, write a brief report to Marlow explaining whether she will be able to repay the $250,000 bank loan at the end of September.

Problem 22.9A
Preparing and Using a Flexible Budget

Eight Flags is a retail department store. The following cost-volume relationships were used in developing a flexible budget for the company for the current year:

	Yearly Fixed Expenses	Variable Expenses per Sales Dollar
Cost of merchandise sold..		$0.65
Selling and promotion expense...................................	$160,000	0.09
Building occupancy expense..	120,000	0.02
Buying expense..	100,000	0.05
Delivery expense..	110,000	0.01
Credit and collection expense.....................................	60,000	0.01
Administrative expense...	300,000	0.02
Totals..	$850,000	$0.85

Management expected to attain a sales level of $20 million during the current year. At the end of the year, the actual results achieved by the company were as follows:

Net sales..	$18,000,000
Cost of goods sold...	11,160,000
Selling and promotion expense.....................................	800,000
Building occupancy expense...	450,000
Buying expense..	720,000
Delivery expense..	200,000
Credit and collection expense.......................................	100,000
Administrative expense...	360,000

Instructions

a. Prepare a schedule comparing the actual results with flexible budget amounts developed for the actual sales volume of $18,000,000. Organize your schedule as a partial multiple-step income statement, ending with operating income. Include separate columns for (1) flexible budget amounts, (2) actual amounts, and (3) any amount over or (under) budget. Use the cost-volume relationships given in the problem to compute the flexible budget amounts.

b. Write a statement evaluating the company's performance in relation to the plan reflected in the flexible budget.

Problem 22.10A
Flexible Budgeting

XL Industries uses department budgets and performance reports in planning and controlling its manufacturing operations. The following annual performance report for the widget production department was presented to the president of the company:

	Budgeted Costs for 4,000 Units Per Unit	Budgeted Costs for 4,000 Units Total	Actual Costs Incurred	Over or (Under) Budget
Variable manufacturing costs:				
Direct materials	$ 25.00	$100,000	$120,000	$20,000
Direct labor	50.00	200,000	210,000	10,000
Indirect labor	12.00	48,000	50,000	2,000
Indirect materials, supplies, etc.	10.00	40,000	43,000	3,000
Total variable manufacturing costs	$ 97.00	$388,000	$423,000	$35,000
Fixed manufacturing costs:				
Lease rental	$ 10.00	$ 40,000	$ 40,000	- 0 -
Salaries of foremen	25.00	100,000	104,000	$ 4,000
Depreciation and other	18.00	72,000	75,000	3,000
Total fixed manufacturing costs	$ 53.00	$212,000	$219,000	$ 7,000
Total manufacturing costs	$150.00	$600,000	$642,000	$42,000

Although a production volume of 4,000 widgets was originally budgeted for the year, the actual volume of production achieved for the year was 5,000 widgets. Direct materials and direct labor are charged to production at actual costs. Factory overhead is applied to production at the predetermined rate of 150% of the actual direct labor cost.

After a quick glance at the performance report showing an unfavorable manufacturing cost variance of $42,000, the president said to the accountant: "Fix this thing so it makes sense. It looks as though our production people really blew the budget. Remember that we exceeded our budgeted production schedule by a significant margin. I want this performance to show a better picture of our ability to control costs."

Instructions
a. Prepare a revised performance report for the year on a flexible budget basis. Use the same format as the production report above, but revise the budgeted cost figures to reflect the actual production level of 5,000 widgets.
b. Briefly comment on XL's ability to control its variable manufacturing costs.
c. What is the amount of over- or underapplied manufacturing overhead for the year? (Note that a standard cost system is not used.)

CHAPTER 23 ALTERNATE PROBLEMS

Problem 23.1A
Understanding Materials Cost Variances

The cost accountant for Blue Pharmaceuticals has informed you that the company's materials quantity variance for the drug Allegro was exactly equal to its materials price variance for the year. The company's normal level of production is 50 batches of Allegro per year. However, due to uncertainties regarding foundation funding, it produced only 25 batches during the current year. Other cost information regarding Allegro's direct materials is as follows:

Standard price per gram of material..	$60
Actual kilograms purchased and used during the year	100 kg
Actual cost of material purchased during the period	$6,000,000
Number of grams per kilogram..	1,000 grams

Instructions
a. Compute Blue's materials price variance.
b. Compute the standard quantity of material allowed per batch of Allegro produced.
c. Why would you not expect Blue to have a large materials quantity variance?

Problem 23.2A
Understanding Materials Cost Variances

Denton's materials quantity variance for the current month was exactly one-half of its materials price variance. Both variances were unfavorable. The company's cost accountant has supplied us with the following standard cost information:

Standard price per pound of material..	$12
Actual pounds purchased and used during the month	800 pounds
Actual cost per pound of material purchased and used........	$15
Actual units manufactured during this month......................	600 units
Normal productive output per month..................................	700 units

Instructions
- a. Compute Denton's materials price variance.
- b. Compute the standard quantity of material allowed for producing 700 units of product.
- c. Record the journal entry to charge work in process for the cost of materials used during the month.
- d. Compute Denton's overhead volume variance if it is twice the amount of its materials quantity variance. Is the volume variance favorable or unfavorable? How do you know?

Problem 23.3A
Computing and Journalizing Cost Variances

Dyelot Industries manufactures dyes and uses cost standards. The concrete produced in 1,000 pound batches; the normal level of production is 500 batches of dye per month. The standard costs per batch are as follows:

		Standard Costs per Batch
Direct materials:		
Various chemicals (1,000 pounds per batch at $0.80/pound)		$ 800
Direct labor:		
Preparation and blending (20 hours per batch at $8.00/hour)		160
Manufacturing overhead:		
Fixed ($150,000 per month ÷ 500 batches)	$300	
Variable (per batch)	20	320
Total standard cost per batch of fertilizer		$2,380

During January, the company temporarily reduced the level of production to 400 batches of dye. Actual costs incurred in January were as follows:

Direct materials (410,000 pounds at $0.75).............................	$307,500
Direct labor (7,950 hours at $7.80/hour)	62,010
Manufacturing overhead	150,490
Total actual costs (400 batches)...	$520,000
Standard cost of 400 batches	
(400 batches x $1,280 per batch)	512,000
Net unfavorable cost variance..	$ 8,000

Instructions
You have been engaged to explain in detail the elements of the $8,000 net unfavorable cost variance and to record the manufacturing costs for January in the company's standard cost accounting system.
   a. As a first step, compute the materials price and quantity variances, the labor rate and efficiency variances, and the overhead spending the volume variances for the month.
   b. Prepare journal entries to record the flow of manufacturing costs through the standard cost system and the related cost variances. Make separate entries to record the costs of direct materials used, direct labor, and manufacturing overhead. Work in Process Inventory is to be debited only with standard costs.

Problem 23.4A
Computing and Journalizing Cost Variances

Latin Silk Products uses standard costs in a process cost system. At the end of the current month, the following information is prepared by the company's cost accountant:

	Direct Materials	Direct Labor	Manufacturing Overhead
Actual costs incurred................................	$108,000	$96,000	$120,000
Standard costs...	100,000	94,000	112,800
Materials price variance (favorable)...........	2,000		
Materials quantity variance (unfavorable)	10,000		
Labor rate variance (favorable).................		6,000	
Labor efficiency variance (unfavorable)...		8,000	
Overhead spending variance (unfavorable)			1,200
Overhead volume variance (unfavorable).			6,000

The total standard cost per unit of finished product is $15. During the current month, 2,000 units were completed and transferred to the finished goods inventory and 18,000 units were sold. The inventory of work in process at the end of the month consists of 3,000 units that are 70% completed. There was no inventory in process at the beginning of the month.

Instructions
a. Prepare journal entries to record all variances and the costs incurred (at standard) in the Work in Process account. Prepare separate compound entries for (1) direct materials, (2) direct labor, and (3) manufacturing overhead.
b. Prepare journal entries to record (1) the transfer of units finished to the Finished Goods Inventory account and (2) the cost of goods sold (at standard) for the month.
c. Assuming that the company operated at 80% of its normal capacity during the current month, what is the amount of the budgeted fixed manufacturing overhead per month?

Problem 23.5A
Computing and Journalizing Cost Variances

Hans Enterprises is a large producer of bird seeds. During June, it produced 160 batches of crow bait. Each batch weights 1,000 pounds. To produce this quantity of output, the company purchased and used 170,000 pounds of direct material at a cost of $816,000. It also incurred direct labor costs of $20,000 for the 2,500 hours worked by employees on the crow bait crew. Manufacturing overhead incurred at the crow bait plant during June totaled $4,200, of which $3,100 was considered fixed. Hans's standard cost information for 1,000-pound batches of crow bait is as follows:

Direct materials standard price	$5.00 per pound
Standard quantity allowed per batch	1,025 pounds
Direct labor standard rate	$8.25 per hour
Standard hours allowed per batch	15 direct labor hours
Fixed overhead budgeted	$3,200 per month
Normal level of production	150 batches per month
Variable overhead application rate	$10.00 per batch
Fixed overhead application rate ($3,300 ÷ 150 batches)	$22.00 per batch
Total overhead application rate	$32.00 per batch

Instructions
a. Compute the materials price and quantity variances.
b. Compute the labor rate and efficiency variances.
c. Compute the manufacturing overhead spending and volume variances.
d. Record the journal entry to charge materials (at standard) to work in process.
e. Record the journal entry to charge direct labor (at standard) to work in process.
f. Record the journal entry to charge manufacturing overhead (at standard) to work in process.
g. Record the journal entry to transfer the 160 batches of crow bait produced in June to finished goods.
h. Record the journal entry to close any over- or underapplied overhead to cost of goods sold.

Problem 23.6A
Computing and Journalizing Cost Variances

Smooth Corporation is a small producer of paint. During June, the company produced 10,000 cases of paint. Each case contains twelve quarts of paint. To achieve this level of production, Smooth purchased and used 34,000 gallons of direct material at a cost of $43,520. It also incurred average direct labor costs of $14 per hour for the 8,300 hours worked in June by its production personnel. Manufacturing overhead for the month totaled $21,000 of which $4,500 was considered fixed. Smooth's standard cost information for each case of paint is as follows:

Direct material standard price	$1.32 per gallon
Standard quantity allowed per case	3.00 gallons
Direct labor standard rate	$15 per hour
Standard hours allowed per case	0.80 direct labor hours
Fixed overhead budgeted	$5,252 per month
Normal level of production	10,100 cases per month
Variable overhead application rate	1.60 per case
Fixed overhead application rate ($5,252 ÷ 10,100 cases)	0.52 per case
Total overhead application rate	$2.12 per case

Instructions
a. Compute the materials price and quantity variances.
b. Compute the labor rate and efficiency variances.
c. Compute the manufacturing overhead spending and volume variances.
d. Prepare the journal entries to:
   1. Charge materials (at standard) to work in process.
   2. Charge direct labor (at standard) to work in process.
   3. Charge manufacturing overhead (at standard) to work in process.
   4. Transfer the cost of the 10,000 cases of synthetic motor oil produced in June to finished goods.
   5. Close any over- or underapplied overhead into the cost of goods sold.

Problem 23.7A
Computing and Journalizing Cost Variances

The accountants for Monoglut, Inc. have developed the following information regarding the standard cost and the actual cost of a product manufactured in March:

	Standard Cost	Actual Cost
Direct materials:		
Standard: 12 ounces at $0.20 per ounce...............	$2.40	
Actual: 13 ounces at $0.22 per ounce..................		$2.86
Direct labor:		
Standard: .60 hours at $12.00 per hour................	7.20	
Actual: .50 hours at $13.00 per hour...................		6.50
Manufacturing overhead:		
Standard: $6,000 fixed cost and $4,000 variable cost for 10,000 units normal monthly volume...	1.00	
Actual: $6,000 fixed cost and $2,540 variable cost for 7,000 units actually produced in March..		1.20
Total unit cost	$10.60	$10.58

Instructions

a. Compute the materials price variance and the material quantity variance, indicating whether each is favorable or unfavorable. Prepare the journal entry to record the cost of direct materials used during March in the Work in Process account (at standard).

b. Compute the labor rate variance and the labor efficiency variance, indicating whether each is favorable or unfavorable. Prepare the journal entry to record the cost of direct labor used during March in the Work in Process account (at standard).

c. Compute the overhead spending variance and the overhead volume variance, indicating whether each is favorable or unfavorable. Prepare the journal entry to assign overhead cost to production in March.

Problem 23.8A
Computing, Journalizing, and Analyzing Cost Variances

Colonial Furniture Co. uses a standard cost system. One of the company's most popular products is a cherry wood desk. The per-unit standard costs of the desk, assuming a "normal" volume of 2,000 units per month, are as follows:

Direct materials, 100 board-feet of wood at $1.50 per foot....................		$150,000
Direct labor, 4 hours at $10.00 per hour.................................		40.00
Manufacturing overhead (applied at $22 per unit)		
Fixed ($20,000 ÷ 2,000 units of normal production)...............	$15.00	
Variable...	8.00	18.00
Total standard unit cost		$208.00

During May, 1,800 desks were scheduled and produced at the following actual unit costs:

Direct materials, 105 feet at $1.40 per foot	$147.00
Direct labor, 4½ hours at $9.00 per hour..................................	40.50
Manufacturing overhead, $34,200 ÷ 1,800 units	19.00
Total actual unit cost...	$206.50

Instructions
a. Compute the following cost variances for the month of May:
   1. Materials price variance.
   2. Materials quantity variance.
   3. Labor rate variance.
   4. Labor efficiency variance.
   5. Overhead spending variance.
   6. Volume variance.
b. Prepare journal entries to assign manufacturing costs to the Work in Process Inventory account and to record cost variances for May. Use separate entries for (1) direct materials, (2) direct labor, and (3) overhead costs.
c. Comment on any significant problems or areas of cost savings revealed by your computation of cost variances. Also comment on any possible casual relationships between significant favorable and unfavorable cost variances.

Problem 23.9A
Understanding Cost Variances: Solving for Missing Data

Viking Corporation has supplied us with the following information:

Standard production costs allowed for actual level of output achieved....................................	$420,000
Variances:	
Total materials variance (favorable).................................	$ 4,000
Total direct labor variance (favorable).............................	1,000
Total overhead variances (unfavorable)...........................	4,200
Other Information:	
Actual units produced...	20,000 units
Normal or expected production..	20,000 units
Actual cost per pound of materials.....................................	$2.50/pound

Direct labor averaged .80 hours per unit produced, which was .05 hours above the standard time allowed per unit produced. Actual total direct labor cost was $224,000.

The materials price variance equals the overhead volume variance. The actual quantity of materials used during the period was 90% of the standard quantity allowed:

Instructions
Compute the following for Viking:
- a. Materials quantity variance.
- b. Standard quantity of materials allowed to produce 20,000 units.
- c. Actual quantity of materials used to produce 20,000 units.
- d. Actual direct labor rate per hour.
- e. Standard direct labor rate per hour.
- f. Labor rate variance.
- g. Labor efficiency variance.
- h. Overhead spending variance.

Problem 23.10A
Understanding Cost Variances: Solving for Missing Data

The Foding's Corporation has supplied us with the following information obtained from its standard cost system in May:

Standard price of direct materials	$7 per pound
Actual price of direct materials	$6 per pound
Standard direct labor rate	$10 per pound
Actual direct labor hours in May	4,000 hours

The following journal entries were made during May with respect to Foding's standard cost system:

Work in Process Inventory (at standard cost)	9,500	
Materials Quantity Variance	1,000	
Direct Materials Inventory (at actual cost)		9,000
Materials Price Variance		1,500
To record the cost of direct materials used in May.		
Work in Process Inventory (at standard cost)	35,000	
Labor Rate Variance	8,000	
Labor Efficiency Variance	5,000	
Direct Labor (at actual cost)		4,800
To record the cost of direct labor charged to production in May.		
Work in Process Inventory (at standard cost)	28,000	
Overhead Spending Variance	3,000	
Overhead Volume Variance		6,000
Manufacturing Overhead (at actual cost)		25,000
To apply overhead to production in May.		

Instructions

a. Determine the actual quantity of materials purchased and used in production during May.
b. Determine the standard quantity of materials allowed for the productive output achieved during May.
c. Determine the actual average direct labor rate in May.
d. Determine the standard direct labor hours allowed the production output achieved during May.
e. Determine the total overhead costs allowed for the production output achieved during May.
f. Prepare a journal entry to record the transfer of all work in process to finished goods at the end of May.
g. Close all cost variances directly to the Cost of Goods Sold account at the end of May.
h. Was Foding's production output in May more or less than its normal level of output? How can you tell?

Problem 23.11A
Understanding Cost Variances: Solving for Missing Data

The Ninna Company manufactures wooden shelves. An accountant for Ninna just finished completing the variance report for the current month. After printing the report, his computer's hard disk crashed, effectively destroying most of the actual results for the month. Al that the accountant remembers is that actual production was 250 shelves and that all materials purchased were used in production. The following information is also available:

Current Month: Budgeted Amounts	
Budgeted production: 225 magazine stands	
Direct materials: Wood	
Usage	4 square feet per shelf
Price	$0.20 per square foot
Direct labor:	
Usage	.4 hours per stand
Rate	$12 per hour
Variable overhead (allocated based on direct labor hours)	
Rate per labor hour	$5
Rate per stand	$2
Fixed overhead (allocated based on direct labor hours)	
Rate per labor hour	$10
Rate per stand	$4
Current Month: Variances	
Direct materials price variance	40 Unfavorable
Direct materials quantity variance	-0-
Direct labor rate variance	200 Favorable
Direct labor efficiency variance	300 Unfavorable
Overhead volume variance	50 Favorable
Overhead spending variance	100 Unfavorable

Instructions
Using the budget for the current month and the variance report, construct the items below:
    a. What was the actual purchase price per square foot of wood?
    b. How many labor hours did it actually take to produce each shelf?
    c. What was the actual wage rate paid per hour?
    d. What was the actual total overhead for the month?

CHAPTER 24 ALTERNATE PROBLEMS

Problem 24.1A
Republic Hotel

The Republic Hotel is a full-service hotel in a large city. Republic is organized into three departments that are treated as investment centers. Budget information for the coming year for these three departments is shown below. The managers of each of the departments are evaluated and bonuses are awarded each year based on ROI.

	Republic Hotel		
	Hotel Rooms	Restaurants	Health Club-Spa
Average investment	$10,000,000	$6,000,000	$1,200,0000
Sales revenue	14,000,000	2,500,000	700,000
Operating expenses	10,000,000	1,100,000	500,000
Operating earnings	4,000,000	1,400,000	200,000

Instructions

a. Compute the ROI for each department. Use the DuPont method to analyze the return on sales and capital turnover.
b. Assume the Health Club-Spa is considering installing new exercise equipment. Upon investigating, the manager of the division finds that the equipment would cost $60,000 and that sales revenue would increase by $10,000 per year as a result of the new equipment. What is the ROI of the investment in the new exercise equipment? What impact does the investment in the exercise equipment have on the Health Club-Spa's ROI? Would the manager of the Health Club-Spa be motivated to undertake such an investment?
c. Compute the residual income for each department if the minimum required return for the Republic Hotel is 18%. What would be the impact of the investment in **b** on the Heatlth Club-Spa's residual income?

Problem 24.2A
Republic Hotel and Balanced Scorecard

Consider the Republic Hotel discussed in Problem 24.1A. The manager of the Restaurants Department complains that sales and resulting earnings for the restaurants are not higher due to the poor reputation of the Hotel Rooms Department. Because the Hotel Rooms Department does not have the best housekeeping staff, the overall reputation of the hotel is slipping. The manager of the Hotel Rooms Department counters that to keep operating expenses under control and improve ROI, wages for housekeeping have been cut. The manager of the Restaurant Department has requested that other evaluation techniques be considered such as residual income or a balanced scorecard approach that might resolve this problem.

Instructions

Consider which balanced scorecard measures might be useful to the Republic Hotel in evaluating the Hotel Rooms Department. In doing so, identify:
   a. The organizational goal that the measure is designed to support.
   b. The employee resources and efforts that will be affected by the measurement.
   c. How the employees should receive feedback and be rewarded for progress toward achieving the goals.

Problem 24.3A
Evaluating Business Unit Performance

The manager of Wilson's Toy Division is evaluated on her division's return on investment and residual income. The company requires that all divisions generate a minimum return on invested assets of 10%. Consistent failure to achieve this minimum target is grounds for the dismissal of a division manager. The annual bonus paid to division managers is 1.5% of residual income in excess of $200,000. The Toy Division's operating margin for the year was $10 million, during which time its average invested capital was $75 million.

Instructions
a. Compute the Toy Division's return on investment and residual income.
b. Will the manager of the Toy Division receive a bonus for her performance? If so, how much will it be?
c. In reporting her investment center's performance for the past 10 years, the manager of the Toy Division accounted for the depreciation of her division's assets by using an accelerated depreciation allowed for tax purposes. As a result, virtually all of the assets under her control are fully depreciated. Given that the company's other division managers use straight-line depreciation, is her use of an accelerated method ethical? Defend your answer.

Problem 24.4A
ROI and Residual Income at Big Deal Inc.

Joe Teller is the manager of one location of the Big Deal Inc. chain. Teller's location is currently earning an ROI of 15% on existing average capital of $800,000. The minimum required return for Big Deal Inc. is 12%. Teller is considering several additional investment projects, which are independent of existing operations and are independent of each other. The following table lists the projects:

Project	Required Capital	ROI
A	$200,000	16.2%
B	400,000	22.0
C	300,000	14.0
D	500,000	12.4
E	600,000	10.0

Instructions
a. Which of the above projects would Teller choose for investment if his objective is to maximize his location's ROI?
b. Which projects increase the value of Big Deal Inc.?
c. Which projects have a negative residual income?
d. Rank the projects in the order of acceptability if Teller is evaluated on ROI and then on residual income.

Problem 24.5A
Balanced Scorecard in the Assembly Department

Sandra Olson manages the Finishing Department at Buildwell machines, a part supplier to large airplane companies. Buildwell has recently adopted a balanced scorecard for the entire company. As a result, the plant manager for each production facility has a set of strategic goals, measurements, and rewards designed to motivate employees to achieve the company's overall goals.

The plant manager has implemented the balanced scorecard throughout each department. The balanced scorecard measures that specifically apply to the Finishing Department are primarily related to business process measures and learning and growth measures. In particular, the assembly line and related employees supervised by Olson are evaluated on efficiency measures and learning and growth measures. The learning and growth measures are employee absenteeism, retention, and satisfaction. Operating efficiencies are measured by cycle time, amount of work-in-process inventory, hours of machine downtime, number of defects, cost of rework, and productivity per employee. Olson obtains a monthly cash bonus if she can increase the learning and growth measures and reduce inefficiencies in the operations.

During the first year that the balanced scorecard was used at Buildwell, Olson did not earn a bonus. She has been particularly frustrated because whenever she reduces the work in process inventory on the shop floor, cycle time increases. When she reduces the hours of machine down-time, the defects increase and employee satisfaction decreases.

The plant manager decides to hire your consulting firm, Knowitall Incorporated, to help evaluate the new balanced scorecard performance measurement and compensation scheme.

Instructions

Choose a partner to round out your consulting team and write a memo to the plant manager that explains the problems the manger is encountering in the Finishing Department. In the report identify with bullet points the problems that she is having with the balanced scorecard system and provide suggestions to the plant manager to help remedy the problems.

CHAPTER 25 ALTERNATE PROBLEMS

Problem 25.1A

Capital Budgeting and Determination of Annual Net Cash Flows

Monster Toys is considering a new toy monster called Garga. Annual sales of Garga are estimated at 100,000 units at a price of $8 per unit. Variable manufacturing costs are estimated at $3 per unit, incremental fixed manufacturing costs (excluding depreciation) at $60,000 annually, and additional selling and general expenses related to the monster at $40,000 annually.

To manufacture the monsters, the company must invest $400,000 in design molds and special equipment. Since toy fads wane in popularity rather quickly, Monster Toys anticipates the special equipment will have a three-year service life with only a $10,000 salvage value. Depreciation will be computed on a straight-line basis. All revenue and expenses other than depreciation will be received or paid in cash. The company's combined federal and state income tax rate is 30%.

Instructions
a. Prepare a schedule showing the estimated increase in annual net income from the planned manufacture and sale of Garga.
b. Compute the annual net cash flows expected from this project.
c. Compute for this project the (1) payback period, (2) return on average investment, and (3) net present value, discounted at an annual rate of 12%. Round the payback period to the nearest tenth of a year and the return on average investment to the nearest tenth of a percent.

Problem 25.2A
Analyzing Capital Investment Proposal

Macro Technology is considering two alternative proposals for modernizing its production facilities. To provide a basis for selection, the cost accounting department has developed the following data regarding the expected annual operating results for the two proposals:

	Proposal 1	Proposal 2
Required investment in equipment	$400,000	$380,000
Estimated service life of equipment	10 years	8 years
Estimated salvage value	$ -0-	$ 20,000
Estimated annual cost savings (net cash flow)	80,000	82,000
Depreciation on equipment (straight-line basis)	40,000	45,000
Estimated increase in annual net income	40,000	56,000

Instructions
a. For each proposal, compute the (1) payback period, (2) return on average investment, and (3) net present value, discounted at an annual rate of 15%. (Round the payback period to the nearest tenth of a year and the return on investment to the nearest tenth of a percent.)
b. Based on your analysis in part **a**, state which proposal you would recommend and explain the reasons for your choice.

Problem 25.3A
Analyzing Capital Investment Proposal

Flagg Equipment Company is evaluating two alternative investment opportunities. The controller of the company has prepared the following analysis of the two investment proposals:

	Proposal A	Proposal B
Required investment in equipment..................................	$260,000	$280,000
Estimated service life of equipment	6 years	7 years
Estimated salvage value	$ 20,000	$ -0-
Estimated annual net cash flow......................................	82,000	65,000
Depreciation on equipment (straight-line basis)	40,000	40,000
Estimated annual net income...	42,000	25,000

Instructions
a. For each proposal investment, compute the (1) payback period, (2) return on average investment, and (3) net present value, discounted at an annual rate of 15%. (Round the payback period to the nearest tenth of a year and the return on investment to the nearest tenth of a percent.)
b. Based on your analysis in part **a**, which proposal do you consider to be the better investment? Explain.

Problem 25.4A
Capital Budgeting Using Multiple Models

Tango is a popular restaurant located in the Brazilton Resort. Management feels that enlarging the facility to incorporate a large outdoor seating area will enable Tango to continue to attract existing customers as well as handle large banquet parties that now must be turned away. Two proposals are currently under consideration. Proposal A involves a temporary walled structure and umbrellas used for sun protection; Proposal B entails a more permanent structure with a full awning cover for use even in inclement weather. Although the useful life of each alternative is estimated to be 10 years, Proposal B results in higher salvage value due to the awning protection. The accounting department of Brazilton Resort and the manager of Tango have assembled the following data regarding the two proposals:

	Proposal A	Proposal B
Required investment..	$250,000	$300,000
Estimated life of fixtures	10 years	10 years
Estimated salvage value	$ 10,000	$ 40,000
Estimated annual net cash flow	75,000	50,000
Depreciation (straight-line basis)	24,000	36,000
Estimated annual net income.......................................	?	?

Instructions
a. For each proposal, compute the (1) payback period, (2) return on average investment, and (3) net present value discounted at management's required rate of 12%. (Round the payback period to the nearest tenth of a year and the return on investment to the nearest tenth of a percent.)
b. Based on your analysis in part **a**, state which proposal you would recommend and explain the reasons for your choice.

Problem 25.5A
Capital Budgeting Using Multiple Models

I.C. Cream is considering two possible expansion plans. Proposal A involves opening 8 stores in northern Alaska at a total cost of $4,000,000. Under another strategy, Proposal B, I.C. Cream would focus on southern Alaska and open five stores for at total cost of $3,000,000. Selected data regarding the two proposals have been assembled by the controller of I.C. Cream as follows:

	Proposal A	Proposal B
Required investment.	$4,000,000	$3,000,000
Estimated life of store locations	8 years	8 years
Estimated salvage value	$ -0-	$ 200,000
Estimated annual net cash flow	800,000	700,000
Depreciation on equipment (straight-line basis)	500,000	350,000
Estimated annual net income	?	?

Instructions
a. For each proposal, compute the (1) payback period, (2) return on average investment, and (3) net present value, discounted at management's required rate of 12%. (Round the payback period to the nearest tenth of a year and the return on investment to the nearest tenth of a percent.)
b. Based on your analysis in part **a**, state which proposal you would recommend and explain the reasoning behind your choice.

Problem 25.6A
Analyzing Capital Investment Proposal

Cafiend Appliance Company is planning to introduce a coffee grinder to its line of small home appliances. Annual sales of the grinder are estimated at 15,000 units at a price of $40 per unit. Variable manufacturing costs are estimated at $18 per unit, incremental fixed manufacturing costs (other than depreciation) at $60,000 annually, and incremental selling and general expenses relating to the grinders at $75,000 annually.

To build the grinders, the company must invest $300,000 in molds, patterns, and special equipment. Since the company expects to change the design of the grinder every five years, this equipment will have a five-year service life with no salvage value. Depreciation will be computed on a straight-line basis. All revenue and expenses other than depreciation will be received or paid in cash. The company's combined state and federal tax rate is 30%.

Instructions
a. Prepare a schedule showing the estimated annual net income from the proposal to manufacture and sell the grinders.
b. Compute the annual net cash flows expected from the proposal.
c. Compute for this proposal the (1) payback period (round to the nearest tenth of a year), (2) return on average investment (round to the nearest tenth of a percent), and (3) net present value, discounted at an annual rate of 12%.

Problem 25.7A
Considering Financial and Nonfinancial Factors

Doctors Mowtain, Lawrence, and Curley are radiologists living in Yukville, Maine. They realize that many of the state's small, rural hospitals cannot afford to purchase their own magnetic resonance imaging devices (MRIs). Thus the doctors are considering whether it would be feasible for them to form a corporation and investment in their own MRI unit. The unit would be transported on a scheduled basis to more than 80 rural hospitals using an 18-wheel tractor-trailer. The cost of a tractor-trailer equipped with MRI equipment is approximately $1,500,000. The estimated life of the investment is nine years, after which time its salvage value is expected to be no more than $200,000.

The doctors anticipate that the investment will general incremental revenue of $900,000 per year. Incremental expenses (which include depreciation, insurance, fuel, maintenance, their salaries, and income taxes) will average $800,000 per year. Net incremental cash flows will be reinvested back into the corporation. The only difference between incremental cash flows and incremental income is attributable to depreciation expense. The doctors require a minimum return on their investment of 15%.

Instructions
a. Compute the payback period of the mobile MRI proposal.
b. Compute the return on average investment of the proposal.
c. Compute the net present value of the proposal using the tables in Chapter 25 of the text.
d. What nonfinancial factors should the doctors consider in making their decisions?

Problem 25.8A
Analyzing Competing Capital Investment Proposals

Madison Mountain is a small ski resort located in Northern Connecticut. In recent years, the resort has experienced two major problems: (1) unusually low annual snowfalls and (2) long lift lines. To remedy these problems, management is considering two investment proposals. The first involves a $150,000 investment in equipment used to make artificial snow. The second involves the $200,000 purchase of a new high-speed chairlift.

The most that the resort can afford to invest at this time is $220,000. Thus it cannot afford to fund both proposals. Choosing one proposal over the other is somewhat problematic. If the resort funds the snowmaking equipment, business will increase, and lift lines will become even longer than they are currently. If it funds the chairlift, lines will be shortened, but there may not be enough natural snow to attract skiers to the mountain.

The following estimates pertain to each of these investment proposals:

	Snowmaking Equipment	Chair Lift
Estimated life of investment..	10 years	20 years
Estimated incremental annual revenue of investment....	$50,000	$60,000
Estimated incremental annual expense of investment (including taxes)...	20,000	22,000

Neither investment is expected to have any salvage value. Furthermore, the only difference between incremental cash flow and incremental income is attributable to depreciation. Due to inherent risks associated with the ski industry and the resort's high cost of capital, a minimum return on investment of 20% is required.

Instructions
a. Compute the payback period of each proposal.
b. Compute the return on average investment of each proposal.
c. Compute the net present value of each proposal using the tables in Chapter 25 of the text.
d. What nonfinancial factors should be considered?
e. Which proposal, if either, do you recommend as a capital investment?

Problem 25.9A
Analyzing Competing Capital Investment Proposals

Boom, Inc. sells business software. Currently, all of its programs come on 3.5-inch floppy disks. Due to their complexity, some of these applications occupy as many as seven disks. Not only are 3.5-inch disks cumbersome for customers to load, they are relatively expensive for Boom to purchase. The company does not intend to discontinue using 3.5-inch disks altogether. However, it does want to reduce its reliance on the floppy disk medium.

Two proposals are being considered. The first is to provide software on laser disks. Doing so requires a $500,000 investment in duplicating equipment. The second is to make software available through a computerized "modem bank." In essence, programs would be downloaded directly from Boom using telecommunication technology. Customers would gain access to Boom's mainframe using a modem, specify the program they wish to order, and provide their name, address, and credit card information. The software would then be transferred directly to the customers' hard drive, and copies of the users' manual and registration material would be mailed the same day. The proposal requires an initial investment of $350,000.

The following information pertains to these proposals. Due to rapidly changing technology, neither proposal is expected to have any salvage value or an estimated life exceeding five years.

	Laser Disk Equipment	Modem Bank Installation
Estimated incremental annual revenue of investment....	$400,000	$260,000
Estimated incremental annual expense of investment (including taxes)...	260,000	140,000

The only difference between Boom's incremental cash flows and its incremental income is attributable to depreciation. A minimum return on investment of 12% is required.

Instructions
a. Compute the payback period of each proposal.
b. Compute the return on average investment of each proposal.
c. Compute the net present value of each proposal using the tables in Chapter 25 of the text.
d. What nonfinancial factors should be considered?
e. Which of Boom's employees would most likely underestimate the benefits of investing in the modem bank? Why?
f. Which proposal, if either, do you recommend Boom choose?

Problem 25.10A
Replacing Existing Equipment

Exitology has noticed a significant decrease in the profitability of its line of VCRs. The production manager believes that the source of the trouble is old, inefficient equipment used to manufacture the product. The issue raised, therefore, is whether Exitology should (1) buy new equipment at a cost of $100,000 or (2) continue using its present equipment.

It is unlikely that demand for these VCRs will extend beyond a five-year time horizon. Thus, Exitology estimates that both the new equipment and the present equipment will have a remaining useful life of five years and no salvage value.

The new equipment is expected to produce annual cash savings in manufacturing costs of $30,000, before taking into consideration depreciation and taxes. However, management does not believe that the use of new equipment will have any effect on sales volume. Thus their decision rests entirely on the magnitude of the potential cost savings.

The old equipment has a book value of $80,000. However, it can be sold for only $10,000 if it is replaced. Exitology has an average tax rate of 30% and uses straight-line depreciation for tax purposes. The company requires a minimum return of 15% on all investments in plant assets.

Instructions
a. Compute the net present value of the new machine using the tables in Chapter 25 of the text.
b. What nonfinancial factors should Exitology consider?
c. If the manager of Exitology is uncertain about the accuracy of the cost savings estimate, what actions could be taken to double-check the estimate?